Saints of Old

Patrick Coffey

iUniverse, Inc.
Bloomington

Saints of Old

The views expressed in this work are solely those of the author and do not necessarily reflect the views of the publisher, and the publisher hereby disclaims any responsibility for them.

iUniverse books may be ordered through booksellers or by contacting:

iUniverse
1663 Liberty Drive
Bloomington, IN 47403
www.iuniverse.com
1-800-Authors (1-800-288-4677)

Because of the dynamic nature of the Internet, any web addresses or links contained in this book may have changed since publication and may no longer be valid.

Any people depicted in stock imagery provided by Thinkstock are models, and such images are being used for illustrative purposes only.

Certain stock imagery © Thinkstock.

ISBN: 978-1-4620-0130-9 (sc)
ISBN: 978-1-4620-0131-6 (ebk)

Printed in the United States of America

iUniverse rev. date: 5/19/2011

Foreword

In this book there are stories about the lives of some Christian saints who lived in the first ten centuries after the birth of Jesus Christ.

My reading about Christian saints happened almost fortuitously. Of course, my interest was small at first but grew. I delved deeper into the lives of many of these saints. I was touched by them. There is beauty in the faith, courage and constancy shown in their lives. They were exceptional. I felt like writing about them.

I was born and grew up in England of Irish/Scottish parents. After schooling, the Second World War being on, I joined the British Navy which found me in the Pacific at the end of and after the war. I became interested in a career in Medicine and was admitted to medical school in Britain. Not long after graduation I was married and my wife and I immigrated to Canada. Later still, I trained in General Surgery and practiced this specialty. My wife and I have four children and ten grandchildren.

We live on the shores of Lake Ontario, and on a clear day we can see a small glimpse of New York State, U.S.A.

Contents

1. The Martyrs of Rome and the Roman Empire . . . 1
2. Early Popes 11
3. Saint Ignatius of Antioch 15
4. Saint Cecilia. 19
5. Saint Agnes 23
6. Saint Helena 25
7. Saint George 29
8. Saint Alban 33
9. Saint Vincent. 37
10. Saint Martin of Tours. 41
11. Saint Nicholas 47
12. Saint Monica 51
13. Saint Augustine of Hippo 55
14. Saint Ambrose 59
15. Saint Jerome 71
16. Saint Patrick 77
17. Saint Brendan 83
18. Appendix to "Saint Brendan". 89
19. Saint Columba. 101
20. Saint Aidan 105
21. Saint Leo (Pope Leo the Great) 109
22. Saint Benedict 111
23. Saint Gregory (Pope Gregory the Great) 117
24. The Venerable Bede (Saint Bede) 121
25. Saint Boniface 125
26. Saint Walburga 130

27. Saint Wenceslas 134
28. Saint Stephen, King of Hungary 138
29. Saint Anselm 144
30. Saint Margaret of Scotland. 150

The Martyrs of Rome and the Roman Empire

Those early Christians of Rome and the Roman Empire, how brave they were! They knew they were in danger of being persecuted, perhaps being put to death by the Roman authorities, if discovered. They had to meet together, pray and practise their faith in secret. In Rome this was in private houses or in the "catacombs", underground places in Rome. (See Endnote 1).

Many of these private houses where Christians met were the homes of prominent citizens of Rome who had become Christians and they had houses large enough to hold many people. They courageously opened their houses for meetings. In fact, these houses became secret churches. Many of these "prominent citizens" later lost their lives as a result of so doing. Some of these citizens were not just affluent but some of them were actually high officials in the court of the current Emperor, and it only took a sudden change from a benign Emperor to a fierce one, and for someone looking for a position in the court to denounce the Christian official to the Emperor, for the official to lose his life as a martyr.

These houses, where it was usual to have meetings and divine services, had to be converted. There was a large room or a hall or an "atrium" for masses, baptisms etc. In this "atrium" there was an altar, which had been consecrated to Christ. There was a raised platform with a desk for the reader. The reader read the Sacred Scriptures from scrolls of papyrus, kept carefully guarded; for all copies of the scrolls had to be written laboriously by hand. There was a pool of water for baptisms. Finally, (and with thanks to the writings of C. Bernard Ruffin for all these details), there was usually an adjoining room for other meetings and meals.

These Christians had their own secret sign, (the symbol of the fish), so as to identify themselves as Christians. This is a very simplified diagram of a fish, able to be drawn with just a few strokes. Why fish? The Greek alphabet letters that spelt the word Fish stood for Jesus Christ, Son of God, Saviour. Or, was it that in those early days, Christians seemed to remember the words of Christ when He told St. Peter the fisherman that he would in future be a "fisher of men"? And, unquestionably, those early Christians were not just disciples, but in important ways were a source of conversion to others.

The early Christians of Rome were put to death in different ways. One way was quite openly in an arena, for the Romans enjoyed watching them being killed by lions in these arenas. One of the most feared Roman emperors was Nero, who was a weak and evil emperor. In the year 64 AD the great fire of Rome occurred, ravaging a great part of the city. It has been said that Nero sat "fiddling with his lyre" ostentatiously while the fire raged. Some suspicion fell on Nero himself as to the cause of the fire. So he strongly accused the Christians of starting it. The great Roman historian of the time, Tacitus, wrote that no one believed that the Christians did this, but, nevertheless, they were persecuted even worse than before. Those faithful Christians suffered cruelly, not only in terms of numbers but also in terms of the savage ways they were put to death. However, Nero's efforts proved fruitless, for the citizens of Rome and the Empire were so impressed by the faith and courage of the martyrs, and so swayed and moved by the story of the life, the miracles and teachings of Jesus Christ that, in time, the martyrs were replaced by men and women who converted to Christianity. (Endnote 2).

In the first three centuries after Christ, until Emperor Constantine ruled that Christianity should no longer be attacked, but tolerated, (312 AD), (Endnote3), it has been estimated that there were about one million men and women who lost their lives as martyrs in the countries of the Roman Empire.

Two of the greatest figures of the New Testament can be named among the early martyrs of Rome. They are the great saints, St. Peter and St. Paul. In fact, they were living in Rome in 64 AD, the time of the great fire of Rome, and were martyred later in the time of Nero.

St. Peter, whose name was originally Simon, was renamed Peter (Petros) by Jesus Christ, because He had chosen him to be the rock (petra) upon which his church would be built. Peter was executed in Rome. It has been said that Peter was crucified, and in deference to his Lord, to whom he considered himself so inferior, and whom he loved so much, chose to be crucified head down. (Endnote 4.)

St. Paul was singled out by Jesus Christ to be his great follower and apostle, like St. Peter. Also, like St. Peter, his named changed. Saul became Paul. He has been called the apostle of the Gentiles. He was fearless and tireless in his apostleship and like St. Peter ended up his life in Rome and became a martyr, (about 66 AD). He was beheaded.

St. Lawrence was one of the most venerated and fondly remembered Roman martyrs of the early church. Not only was he greatly admired during his lifetime for his energy, courage, his dedication to Christ, and his "soft heart" for the poor of Rome, but he was notably honoured after his death, showing the esteem in which he has been held. Emperor Constantine was the first to build a small church over the place where St. Lawrence was buried, and this was enlarged and made more beautiful by Pope Pelagius in the late 500s AD. The building was further added to until it became a basilica. This Basilica of San Lorenzo (St. Lawrence) remains to this day. Numerous churches, over the centuries and in different countries have been named after this saint.

Lawrence was the chief deacon of Pope Sixtus11. When this pope (and saint) was arrested by the police of Emperor Valerian, (258 AD), Lawrence rushed to where the authorities held Pope Sixtus, greatly concerned, for he was devoted to Sixtus. Lawrence asked the pope, "Where are you going without your son and deacon?"

And, Sixtus replied, "I am not abandoning you, my son, for you will follow me in three days, for greater strife is awaiting you".

St. Lawrence did not go away and hide from the authorities. During those three days he was approached by the prefect of the police and ordered to hand over the finances of the church. Lawrence indicated that they would find the money amongst the poor, for he had already distributed this money to them. St. Lawrence did suffer the same fate as his pope three days later, as foretold, but it is said that he was tortured to death. (Dear readers, I will spare you the details!). St. Lawrence is the patron of the Poor. It is fitting.

It is remembered that the "poor" in that day and age meant the ultra-poor, such as those who were near starvation; and the only way the many beggars could stay alive was by a sufficiently generous response to their begging.

One reads more about male than female martyrs of the first few centuries. This is because men tended to hold the leadership positions--popes, bishops, priests and deacons-- and during a persecution they were targeted first. But there were numerous heroic women martyrs. For instance, one can mention St. Agnes, St. Lucy, St. Cecilia and St. Agatha and there were many others.

And then there is the story of two other notable female saints, St. Perpetua and St. Felicity. We have a record of these two saints in a text named "Passion of St. Perpetua, St. Felicity and their Companions". Perpetua and Felicity and four of the "companions" were arrested and imprisoned for being Christian and refusing to renounce their faith. Part of this "Passion"was written by

St. Perpetua herself, who kept a diary during all the time she was imprisoned; and part by one of the "companions", (Saturus); and part of it was written by an eye-witness to the death of the martyrs. St. Perpetua's account is historical; it is the earliest surviving text written by a Christian woman. This "Passion" story is very moving and very long, but thoroughly worth reading. (My account of the story is very much shortened).

These two women lived early in the Christian era, (they died on March 7th 203). They lived in North Africa in a Roman province called Carthage. (They were venerated in Carthage later by a magnificent church (basilica) built over their tombs).

At the time of their deaths, Perpetua was 22 years old. She was of "noble birth". Her father was an important citizen of the city. He was not a Christian but Perpetua herself was, and her mother and two brothers were. Perpetua was married and had recently given birth to a baby at the time of her arrest.

All we know of Felicity is that she was a young woman, a slave, and she was pregnant, expecting a baby soon at the time of her arrest.

Perpetua was an unusually bright, well-educated, courageous and spiritual person. She was the eldest of the family and much beloved by them. She and Felicity and four others were arrested for openly being Christian and refusing to change. The prison was overcrowded and unbearably hot, but what made the suffering far worse for Perpetua was the worry about her baby. Perpetua's mother, with the help of Christian deacons, who bribed a guard, managed to get Perpetua's baby into the prison where her daughter was. Perpetua was so happy to see and care for her baby that she wrote in her diary, "Suddenly, the prison was made a palace for me". Later, her mother had to steal into the prison again and take the baby back to her home.

Perpetua's vivid account described their sufferings in prison and also told of her father's visits and his desperate and angry attempts to persuade his daughter to renounce Christianity. Her attempt to try and explain her feelings to her father showed not only how resolute she was but also how articulate, because in answer to his entreaty, she pointed to a water jug and asked, "Can you call this by any other name than what it is?" Her father answered, "Of course not". Perpetua went on, "Neither can I call myself by any name than what I am--a Christian".

She had visions and dreams which she recorded in her account. Felicity and some of the other companions also did. These helped in strengthening their courage. In one vision or dream Perpetua saw a ladder leading up to Heaven and at the bottom of the ladder there was a serpent attacking the Christians and trying to prevent them from climbing up the ladder. Perpetua saw this as a sign that she would not just be fighting the wild animals in the arena, but she would also be fighting Satan with his cunning attempts to weaken her resolution.

Felicity, being pregnant, could not be martyred, according to the Roman law. But, not long before her death, she gave birth and the baby was immediately adopted by a Christian woman.

Perpetua, Felicity and three others were tried. (One of their companions had already died in prison). All five bravely confessed their Christian faith. Out of love for Jesus Christ, they could not bring themselves to sacrifice to the Roman gods. It was the gods Saturn and Ceres they were required to worship. So, they were condemned to die, and on the day of the "Games", they were placed in an arena where crowds watched them being killed by the beasts. It is written that Pepetua and Felicity gave each other "the kiss of peace" before they died. It is clear that they grew to love each other dearly during those last weeks of their lives.

The jailers from the prison and the members of the public watching in the arena were overwhelmed, seeing the lack of fear of the martyrs, even when they were attacked by the animals. As a result, many of these either became converts or at any rate became favourably disposed towards Christianity. They began to recognise the strength of the Christians.

Perpetua's tongue did not desert her. Rather, she seemed to be inspired by the situation she was in. When those in charge in the arena tried to force her and the other to dress in the special robes dedicated to the pagan gods, she challenged the executioners, saying, "We came to die out of our own free will, so we will not lose our freedom to worship our God. We gave you our lives so that we wouldn't have to worship your gods". She and the others were allowed to keep on their own clothes.

We do not read much about Felicity in this account. But, her name and that of Perpetua are always so closely linked that she must have shown the same outstanding courage and faith as Perpetua . These two saints are mentioned (commemorated) by name in the[1] Canon of the Mass. Their feast day in the Catholic Church, the Episcopal (Anglican) Church and in the Lutheran Church is remembered on March 7th.

Endnotes

1. The catacombs, the underground passages and galleries, were used by Christians as places of safety from the authorities and as cemeteries, but were barely used after the first three centuries AD. But they were explored by archaeologists in the 15th century and found to contain paintings and inscriptions on the walls, allusions to Abraham, Noah, Moses, Christ's baptism, the resurrection of Lazarus, the Last Supper etc.

2. The Roman Emperors and Caesars varied between some being cruel and self-indulgent in the extreme, (for instance with sex orgies and feast orgies), and others being wise and benign rulers. Some Emperors considered themselves gods and expected to be worshiped.

3. It was not until Constantine the Great became Emperor of Rome that persecution of Christians ceased all over the Roman empire, (Constantine's decree of 312 AD.) In the year 312 AD Constantine won the famous battle of Mylvian Bridge and it has been said that before the battle he saw, in the sky, the Christian cross.

4. After his death, St. Peter was buried at the foot of Vatican Hill. Three centuries later, Emperor Constantine built a church over the site which was later replaced by the present St. Peter's Basilica of Rome.

Early Popes

An extraordinary number of early popes lost their lives and were martyred for their faith. But then, of course, it can be said that all those early Christians risked their lives by simply being called Christian, members of this new religion. It is true that those who stood out as leaders were more in danger. Yes. Of those first five popes, four were certainly martyred and one, Linus, probably so. The last pope to be martyred was Pope St. Martin 1, (but not to be confused with St. Martin of Tours, who was born about 316). Pope St. Martin became pope in 649 and died in 655.

St. Peter. He is often called the first pope. He was not called as such in his lifetime. In fact, the "Pontificate" was somewhat unstructured in its early years, compared to what it became. The leaders of the early Church tended to be called Bishops of Rome. The first pope to use the title "pope" consistently was Pope Siricius who was pope from 384 to 399. What does "Pope" mean? It means "father" and is derived from "papa" (Latin), or "pappas" (Greek). St. Peter was undoubtedly the leader whom Jesus Christ appointed and who spent the last few years of his life, (we are not sure just how many), in Rome, where he was martyred.

It seems from the Gospels that, of the apostles, Peter was the one who was in the forefront during Christ's life on earth. And, it was Peter that Christ asked, not just once, but three times, "Do you love me"? Peter answered in the affirmative of course. A triple question or saying, in the custom of the day, signified the great importance of that question or saying.

Jesus Christ once asked his disciples who people were saying that he was. Various answers were given. But then Peter spoke up, spontaneously and speaking for himself, and said "You are the Messiah, Son of the living God". It was a little after this that Christ said, "You are Peter and on this Rock I will build my Church and............". (St. Mathew, chapter 16, verses 15-20).

It has been said that the first pope whom anything definite is known about was Clement, the fourth pope. Interestingly, his name is spoken in Mass, in the canon. Also, of interest, the Roman historian Tertullian wrote (c199) that Clement was ordained a priest by St. Peter, and that great writer, St. Jerome, who lived from 340 to 420, wrote that Clement worked with St. Paul in Rome.

Pope St. Clement's best-known letter, written when he was pope, was to the Christians in Corinth and was a long letter which tells us something of the character of St. Clement. In the latter part of the letter, Clement praises saints Peter and Paul as, "the greatest and most upright pillars of the church, who were persecuted and struggled unto death". Further in this letter, he wrote, "We are writing this, beloved, not only for your admonition but also as a reminder to ourselves; for, we are placed in the same arena, and the same contest lies before us. Hence, we ought to put aside vain and useless concerns and should consider what is good, pleasing and acceptable in the sight of Him who made us. Let us fix our gaze on the blood of Christ, realising how precious it is to his Father, since it was shed for our salvation and brought the grace of repentance to all the world".

St. Clement is often remembered by an anchor. For, he met his death by being thrown into the sea with an anchor tied to his body.

Fabian, was an early and outstanding pope. The historian, Eusubius, (and also others), has left us an account of Fabian's life. Eusubius relates that when Pope Anterus died, a number of Christians came to Rome to elect a new pope. Fabian was one of these, but he was not one of the notables in the assembly. It happened that during the meeting a dove descended from the ceiling and alighted on the head of Fabian. The men gathered there took this to be a sign from Heaven and Fabian was elected. No doubt they remembered the description of Jesus Christ being baptised by John the Baptist, written in three of the four Gospels. In Christianity the dove has become a symbol of the Holy Spirit.

Fabian was pope longer than usual for those times. The Roman Emperor of the time, Philip, was friendly to the Christians. Fabian accomplished a great deal while he was pope including sending out seven bishops with their helpers as "apostles to the Gauls", (France). Emperor Philip died and his successor ordered that all Christians should deny Christ and instead offer incense to idols. Fabian refused and so lost his life. He was buried in the catacombs and one can still see there the stone slab with his name on it.

St. Fabian left a Prayer, "It's so easy to believe that peace means a life without conflict or suffering. Help us to see that the only true peace is the peace Christ brings. Never let us as a Church or as individual Christians choose to deny our beliefs simply to avoid an unpleasant situation. Amen".

Then, Pope Sixtus was pope for less than a year, from August 31st 257 to August 6th 258. Yes; one of the occupational hazards of being a pope in that era was execution! The Roman Emperor Valerian issued an even stricter and more cruel edict against Christians in 258, ordering that all Christian bishops, priests and deacons be immediately put to death.

The Roman historian Pontius described St. Sixtus as a "good and peaceable priest". The persecution, being so great, Sixtus decided to hold a religious meeting and a mass in a catacomb in Rome where it was difficult to be discovered by the authorities, but they were found. It is said that as soon as the police arrived Sixtus offered himself up in order to prevent the arrest of many others. But he and six of his deacons were taken away and martyred. Before they were taken away, St. Lawrence, a friend and devoted follower of Pope Sixtus, on hearing that Sixtus had been arrested, rushed over to where he was, and the short conversation that the two of them had before Sixtus was taken off is described in "The Martyrs of Rome and the Roman Empire" of this book.

Saint Ignatius of Antioch

St Ignatius of Antioch was a convert to Christianity, a dedicated follower of Christ, a bishop and a martyr, who lived not long after Christ and was a contemporary of St. Peter, St. Paul and many other illustrious saints. (It is easy to confuse him with anther Ignatius, St. Ignatius of Loyola, the founder of the Jesuits, who lived in the 1500s).

Ignatius was born in Syria and it is uncertain just when, but probably between 35 and 50 AD. Since then, there have been stories about him, one of the famous ones being that he was the child whom Jesus took up in his arms as described in St. Mark's Gospel, chapter 9, verse 35.

What is more certain is that Ignatius almost certainly knew and came under the influence of no less a person than St. John the Evangelist, often known as the beloved disciple of Christ, who lived to a great age.

Ignatius became the Bishop of Antioch, in Syria, and was bishop for many years. He was greatly loved and his fame spread widely. It was when he had been bishop for about 40 years that the Roman Emperor of the day, Trajan, who had just waged a successful war not far from Syria, and "flushed with his success", decided to stamp out Christianity. Ignatius was an obvious Christian leader and he was summoned to present himself to the Emperor. It has been reported, with admiration, that Ignatius spoke eloquently and courageously to the Emperor, utterly refusing to renounce his Christian faith. So, off he was sent to Rome for his penalty; he was devoured by lions in the Flavian amphitheatre as soon as he reached Rome.

It is touching to read the story of the voyage Ignatius took between Syria and Rome, during which he was bound in chains and brutally treated by his captors, as he himself wrote. At every port the ship called at during this voyage, he was greeted by crowds of Christians. Word had spread. It is worthy of note that when the ship bound for Rome reached Smyrna, Polycarp (St. Polycarp) who was bishop of Smyrna at the time met his old friend Ignatius. Everyone knew what was to befall him when he reached Rome.

Ignatius and Polycarp had known each other for many years and, in fact, there is not much doubt but that they had both listened to the teaching of St. John the Evangelist when they were young. Perhaps they had run into each other then. Like Ignatius, Polycarp had been an exceptionally devoted bishop, showing an example of courage in the face of the cruel persecution by the anti-Christian forces, who were determined to wipe out this new religion. And also, he battled various heresies with their false beliefs. Later, Polycarp himself was martyred, (at the age of 86). It must have been a heart-felt meeting when these two met in Smyrna. Before he died Ignatius wrote a letter to Polycarp, (still in existence).

It has been said that so great was Ignatius' devotion to Christ that he tried to imitate Him throughout his life, and when it came time for his martyrdom he seemed to welcome the chance to give up his life for Christ.

During the voyage to Rome, Ignatius wrote, (probably partly dictated), seven famous letters. The letter to Polycarp was the only personal letter. The others were written to Christians in different centres, such as in Rome, Ephesus etc. These seven have been authenticated as having been written by him. The seven letters, still preserved, have been so greatly admired that one author wrote, "They were counted among the treasures of early Christianity". One remembers that these were written only a hundred or so years after the birth of Christ, and one is amazed how far the Church's teachings had developed and become solidified after that short period of time. The following are some of the important points the saint raised in these letters:

1. The value of Christ's presence in the Eucharist.
2. Loyalty of the Christian people to their bishop.
3. The Church was divinely established with the salvation of souls as its end.
4. The religious character of matrimony.
5. The primacy of Rome as the centre.
6. The holiness of the Church. The infallibility of the Church. The catholicity of the Church.

Saint Cecilia

St. Cecilia was not just a canonised saint, but she was also a martyr. Like so many of the saints of the early centuries after Christ she gave up her life rather than renounce her Christian faith. She was painfully put to death about AD 230, (but some researchers have put it earlier than this). Speaking about martyrs, the author C. Bernard Ruffin wrote in his book that it has been estimated that about one million men and women in the countries around the Mediterranean were martyred in the first three centuries AD. Perhaps it was because of the proximity in time to when Christ lived and died; the stories and memories of Christ were not old. Also, the authorities in charge at that time were often cruel tyrants and wanted to stamp out this new "atheistic" religion.

To a great number of people the name St. Cecilia makes them think right away of music. She has been the patron saint of musicians since she died.

Cecilia was born into a family whose forbears were fairly important citizens of Rome. She wished to give her life to Christ as a virgin, but her father insisted that she got married and chose a very likable young man from an affluent family in Rome by the name of Valerian.

Before they were married and as they got to know each other, Cecilia confided to Valerian that she had become a Christian. In fact, she had become a devout one. She had studied the Gospels without making this known to her father and had memorised part of them. Practising Christian penance, she wore the very uncomfortable hair shirt under her expensive outer clothing. Cecilia expressed her love for Christ and her faith in Him to Valerian, and also her fervent wish that he, Valerian, would become a Christian. In fact, she went as far as to state that she would not marry him unless he converted. It is not certain whether it was the fact that Valerian was won over to Christianity by Cecilia's obvious sincere faith, or whether he had become so much in love with Cecilia that he could not bear to be parted from her, but he lost no time in seeing a Christian bishop and being baptised a Christian. They were married.

Valerian became not just a nominal Christian, but, like his wife, a devout one. His arguments and testimony and those of his wife convinced his brother to join him, and he was baptised as well.

Valerian and his brother were obviously exceptional individuals. The two of them undertook the unpleasant but important task of giving proper burial to the Christian martyrs who had lost their lives and whose bodies were lying around unburied. They were buried on property belonging to Cecilia. Cecilia and Valerian opened their large house to be used as a church. Cecilia's apostolic zeal and powers of persuasion resulted in the conversion of many. Later, the work of Valerian and his brother, carrying the bodies of martyrs to the cemetery for burial, was reported to the authorities. The brothers were arrested and became martyrs themselves. Their attitude and behaviour before they were beheaded was exemplary, and one Roman soldier who was present could not contain his emotions and admiration for the Christian men, and that sealed his doom.

Cecilia, as a widow, continued to have her house used as a church and the time came when she was arrested and ordered to sacrifice to the pagan gods. She refused and was condemned to death. I will not go into the details of this, but just say that the loathsome attempts to put her to death by torture were botched and it took three days for her to die. Other prisoners around her were convinced she was a saint after she finally died.

How is it that St. Cecilia is associated so strongly with music? We know so little about the events of her life that all we have are a few vague writings such as that at the time of her marriage to Valerian, she was "singing praises to God from her heart", and that "she was singing divine praises before she died". But, it is certain that she left a reputation for having had a love of music and for playing music. One has to assume that she was an exceptionally talented player of music. This is shown by the fact that in the Middle Ages many musical festivals or concerts were celebrated in her honour and innumerable church windows and paintings by famous painters depict her playing the organ or some musical instrument. She is remembered as a musician by great writers such as Chaucer and John Dryden. Musicians such as Handel, Britten and Purcell have composed music in her honour.

But, the main reason she is still remembered and loved, (since the 3rd century), is because she was heroically saintly to a high degree.

Saint Agnes

St. Agnes, (sometimes pronounced and spelt St. Inez), was a Christian girl in a hostile Roman world. She was probably born in Rome in the early part of the 4th century. Her parents were Christian. She was renowned for having an extraordinarily deep love for Jesus Christ. She was also renowned for her beauty, and because of this, had many male admirers.

It has been said that Agnes was only 13 years old when she died; therefore, if that is so, it has to be assumed that her looks, deportment and manners were those of a woman much more mature than the average 13 year old in today's world. But it is true to say that in those times, women often did get married very young.

Not only did Agnes refuse marriage to her many admirers, but also she had made a promise of chastity to Christ; and this she kept.

Different accounts have been written concerning the last days of Agnes' life. In one of them it is written that one of her suitors was a young man by the name of Procop, who was the son of the Governor. In spite of Procop's gifts and entreaties, Agnes not only refused his proposals of marriage but also resisted all his advances. Procop became very angry and reported to his father that Agnes was a Christian. At first, his father tried to talk Agnes out of remaining a Christian by promising her lavish gifts. But nothing would shake Agnes' adherence to Christ. The Governor changed his tactics and had Agnes put in chains and treated roughly. This made no difference, and, in fact, Agnes remained sublime, calm . In exasperation, the Governor took the extremely cruel step of having Agnes dragged through the streets, without her clothes on, to a brothel. It is said that she was protected by an angel there. Finally she was condemned to death. Even pagan, non-Christians cried openly seeing the lovely girl going to her execution--a beheading.

Since the Middle Ages, Agnes has been pictured holding a lamb, as a symbol of virginal innocence.

She is patron saint of chastity, gardeners, engaged couples, rape victims and virgins.

The feast of St. Agnes has been celebrated on January 21 since the 4th century.

She is, to this day, venerated in the Roman Catholic Church, the Anglican Church, the Eastern Catholic Churches, and the Eastern Orthodox Church. She is commemorated, by name, in the Canon of the Mass.

Saint Helena

St. Helena lived the early part of her life, (born about the middle of the 3rd century), at the time when Christians were persecuted all over the Roman Empire.

Then, Constantine became the Roman Emperor. He is one of the few Roman emperors that historians have called "Great". Constantine won the battle of Melvin Bridge in the year 312. According to legend, during the battle he saw a vision of Christ on the cross in the sky. Following the battle, he made public his decision that from then on Christianity would be tolerated and not persecuted. Towards the end of his life Constantine himself became a baptised Christian.

Why are we writing so much about Emperor Constantine? It is because his mother was St. Helena.

Actually, it appears that Constantine's decision that Christianity should be tolerated and not persecuted was not because of his mother's influence on him, because Helena became a Christian fairly late in life. As soon as she started to become attracted to Christianity, she lost no time in studying, understanding and absorbing it, and she became a great and devoted follower of Jesus Christ. Hers was a strong conversion.

Helena came of humble parents. When she was young she met and married a young Roman soldier. He was ambitious and talented and advanced rapidly in the Roman army. He eventually left Helena and married a well-connected woman to further his political career and rose to the top. Their only son, Constantine, stayed with his mother Helena, and in later life, like his father, he advanced in political life, He became Emperor. He then elevated his mother to a noble position and rank.

Helena did not allow this elevation to go to her head. Just the opposite. Her Christian faith was that strong that she spent her life, till she died at about the age of 80, doing her best to spread Christianity and personally, to continue to follow Christ.

We have the writings of historian Eusebius to thank for telling us much of what St. Helena did. In his writings he described how she became "such a devout servant of God that one might believe her to have been from her very childhood a disciple of the Redeemer of mankind". Others wrote about her too, notably St. Ambrose of Milan. Her son, Emperor Constantine was so devoted to her that he honoured his mother by having coins struck with her effigy on the coins. And, some of these coins are still in existence. But, Helena's ambitions lay in a different direction altogether.

With the coming of legalised Christianity, when masses and services no longer had to be carried out in secret, for fear of being found out by the authorities, Christian churches were being built. Helena was responsible for the building of some of these in and outside Rome. But, to quote a biographer, "The poor and destitute were the special objects of her charity".

Like many devout Christians, she decided on making the arduous journey to the Holy Land, (a pilgrimage). These pilgrims wanted to do something to express their devotion to Christ, for instance to visit where He was born and where He died.

Helena did this at an advanced age. She could have sat back and basked in the glory of being the mother of the Emperor, but she chose otherwise. Pilgrimages to the Holy Land were not easy. It meant, when travelling on land either walking or going on horseback or perhaps travelling in a cart drawn by an ox or a horse, and if on sea, (across the Mediterranean), sailing in primitive vessels. Unlike the "Titanic" these vessels were not touted as being "unsinkable"! In fact, many of them met a grievous end in storms.

It appears that Helena spent a considerable time in the Holy Land in the latter part of her life. She worked hard, and, of course, in her high position she had the resources to do such things as to instigate the building of churches. She built one in Bethlehem, close to the stable or grotto where Jesus Christ was born; and another place that was decided on for a church was on the "Mount of the Ascension" near Jerusalem. She helped to decorate and make beautiful the grotto where Jesus Christ was born. There is the story that Helena and her helpers spent a considerable time looking for the actual cross that Christ was crucified on and found it.

It is not possible to chronicle all the good deeds that resulted from the love Helena had for Christ and his emerging church. She was revered as a saint in her lifetime.

Saint George

St. George. Right away that name conjures up the patron saint of England. Actually, St. George is the patron saint of numerous other countries as well. Or, his name may make you think of the man shown in pictures, clothed in knight's armour, riding on a white horse, slaying a dragon with a long lance!

Of course, this latter image of him is a myth, derived in an imaginative way from the fact that George, in real life, was famous for being a brave soldier.

Yes. George certainly was a brave soldier, but there was more to him than that. He had in him the "stuff" that saints are made of. He had become a faithful follower of Jesus Christ before he became a soldier of the Roman Emperor, and remained so afterwards. And, on a day when the Roman Emperor of the time, Diocletian, decreed that all Roman soldiers were required to worship no other than pagan images, George refused. His faith and courage were so strong that he was executed rather than renounce his Christian faith. More about this later.

In the study of St. George, some have demonstrated a lack of strict historical evidence as opposed to traditional evidence, regarding the events ascribed to him. But, there is evidence of so much veneration and admiration for George, as a saint and a heroic martyr, in nearly every country in Europe, especially in the Eastern European countries for several centuries after his death, that this clearly validates his reputation as a saint. This evidence is in the form of paintings, statues, and churches built and named after him. For instance--mentioning just one country--the historian Bagrationi, writing in the 18th century, estimated that 365 Orthodox churches had been built in Georgia named "St. George". (See Endnote.)

George was born between 275 and 285 AD in a place called Lydda, (Palestine). His parents were Christian and brought him up as such. They were both from noble families. His father, Geronzio, was an important official in the Roman army. He died when George was only 14 and his mother died a few years later. Not long after this, George decided to become a soldier in the Roman army like his father. It so happened that the Roman Emperor, Diocletian, was not far away at the time and George went and presented himself personally to him. The Emperor remembered George's father whom he esteemed highly and welcomed George into the Roman army.

George did very well in the army and was promoted up to the rank of a tribune. Then, in the year 302 AD the Emperor issued an edict stating that every soldier in the army should offer a sacrifice to the pagan gods. George refused. He was considered such a valuable soldier that he was offered bribes in the form of money and land if he would covert to the pagan gods. He continued to refuse.

Because of this, he was condemned to death, an execution preceded by torture. George gave away his possessions to the poor before he died. I will not go into the terrible details of the torturing before he died. It is said that a pagan priest who witnessed the way the saint died made him convert to Christianity. St. George's body was returned to Lydda, the place where he was born, for burial and where Christians soon came to honour him as a martyr.

Endnote

The Roman Catholic Church honours the saint with a feast day on April 23rd, the day he died. In 1963 the Roman Catholic Church, because of a lack of strict historical evidence, demoted St. George to a third class minor saint and removed his name from the Universal Calendar, but retained it in local calendars. Then, after study, in the year 2000, Pope John Paul 11 restored St. George to the Universal Calendar. St. George is very much honoured in the Eastern Orthodox Church, in which he is referred to as a "Great Martyr". The Russian Orthodox Church honours the saint with a feast day on April 23rd and also on two other days in the year.

Saint Alban

St. Alban was the first recorded Christian to be martyred for his faith in Britain. No doubt there were other heroic Christians in Britain, either living about the time of Alban or before him, who also refused to bow down and worship pagan gods, but we have no record of them. Alban was particularly heroic and he has been fondly remembered since he died.

We do not know when he was born and different authorities have given probable dates for his death, namely 209 or 251 or 304 AD. He lived during the time that the Romans occupied Britain, and during the time when Christians were persecuted. He lived and died in a town which went by the Roman name of Verulamium, later renamed in the martyr's honour--St. Albans, (which is in Hertfordshire, England). Although there is uncertainty about the year he was born and the year he died, yet there is sound historical evidence for the fact that Alban, a devout convert to Christianity, gave up his life as a martyr rather than renounce his faith. And, there is also sound historical evidence that he was greatly revered after his death, not only in and around Verulamium, but even extending to certain parts of Europe; and he is still commemorated today.

In the time that Alban lived, there were comparatively few Christians in Britain. Paganism was the dominant religion. The bulk of Christian conversion in Britain took place later. First, this was thanks to the arrival of St. Augustine of Canterbury and his 40 monks into the south of Britain; (they came from Rome in 595); and secondly, it was due to the work of such men as St. Aidan and King Oswald of Northumbria in the north. (St. Aidan founded the Lindisfarne monastery in 635); and also, it was due to the many monks who spread Christianity from even further north than Northumbria--from the monastery of Iona.

The story of St. Alban's conversion to Christianity and his death (martyrdom) mostly comes from the pen of the famous, well-respected historian, the Venerable Bede, (St. Bede). We also hear about him from other sources. Bede's story goes thus.

Alban lived in Verulamium. He was a pagan. It was at a time when persecution of Christians was especially fierce, that a Christian priest, flying for his life from the Roman authorities, came to the house of Alban and Alban took him in. It was for several days that the priest was hidden in Alban's house before the soldiers arrived. During that time Alban got to know the priest well and he was struck by the priest's love of his Christian faith and by his courage. He was instructed in the faith by the priest and then asked to be baptised a Christian; and so this was done. We only have the bare bones of Bede's story, but it is easy to surmise that Alban had already been somewhat drawn towards the Christian faith prior to the arrival of the priest, because he placed himself in definite danger hiding him. And also, one asks oneself the question, why did the priest come "knocking on the door" of Alban's house when he was being pursued. Probably he either knew Alban or knew about him.

While the priest was being sheltered in the home of Alban, it happened that Alban suddenly became aware of the approach of the Roman soldiers. He hurriedly took a heroic step. He put on the cloak of the priest and presented himself as the man they were looking for, the priest. He was arrested and taken to the authorities. When it was discovered that he was not the priest, the judge was infuriated. This had give time for the priest to escape. He ordered that Alban be flogged and after this, hearing that Alban was a Christian, warned him that he had to bow down and offer sacrifice to the pagan gods or else he would be executed. Alban refused to do this. (Incidentally, it is recorded that the priest was found and arrested a few days later and met his death as a martyr.)

St. Alban was taken across the river Ver to the top of a hill for his execution. He was accompanied by his escorts and a large crowd of men and women. Some wondrous stories or legends have come down through the course of time concerning what happened during this walk to the top of the hill and also concerning the last minutes before Alban's death--by beheading. Alban's calm and courageous attitude was impressive. One of these stories is from the writing of Bede himself. It was written that the executioner appointed to carry out the beheading, at the last minute, dropped his sword and refused to carry out the execution. He was perhaps a secret Christian or a would-be Christian. Punishment, in those days was swift, arbitrary and ruthless. Another executioner was chosen and not only Alban, but also the first executioner was beheaded.

Before long, at the place on top of the hill where Alban was executed there arose a small insignificant structure to honour the saint. It had to be built in a subdued manner since there was still persecution of Christians going on. But when the Roman Emperor Constantine decreed that Christianity should be tolerated, (in 312), a small church was built; and later, an "Abbey Church" was built by King Offa of Mercia in 793. This was the precursor of the presently standing St. Alban's Abbey (or Cathedral).

Regarding this "small church, built in 312", St. Bede, the historian had something to say about it when he wrote that this church was a worthy memorial of Alban's martyrdom. He went on to say, "To this day, sick people are healed in this place and the working of frequent miracles continues to bring renown."

There are many churches in England named after St. Alban, and even some outside England, one being the St. Alban's church in Copenhagen, Denmark. Also, the site where St. Alban suffered death became a place of pilgrimage. It is recorded that the great St. Germanus of Auxerre, (sometimes spelt St. Germain), was a pilgrim there in 429.

Saint Vincent

St. Vincent lived in the latter part of the 3rd century and just into the 4th century. He died in 304. We know very little about his life but we do know that he was one of the many martyrs of that era when Christians were persecuted mercilessly. Our admiration goes out to the many men and women who had enough faith and courage to be ready to die for Christ rather than renounce Him.

St. Vincent was born in Saragossa, (sometimes spelt Zaragosa), the main city of the part of Spain known as Aragon, situated in the north east of the country. He was a sincere Christian and joined the church in Saragossa. The bishop of Saragossa, (Bishop Valerian), soon took note of Vincent and placed more and more confidence in him over time. Vincent was ordained a deacon. Deacons were responsible for the church's works of charity and relief for the poor, most commonly the only organised relief there was. The elderly Bishop Valerian had some problems with speaking and preaching after having suffered a stroke and Vincent took over many of the preaching duties of the diocese. Vincent excelled at all he did and he became known to the Roman authorities. This was, of course, dangerous work and it became especially dangerous when the persecution of Christians was very intense under the Governor of that region, Dacian by name, who was strongly anti-Christian. Dacian, arrested both Vincent and Bishop Valerian and they were dragged in chains along the roads to Valencia, (situated on the East coast of Spain).

The bishop and Vincent were kept in prison a long time in Valencia. Then, when it was clear that the old bishop would never change, he was killed. Vincent was subjected to the cruellest of tortures in order to try and get him to renounce his Christianity. He suffered the rack, the grid-iron and scourging. He was put in a cell where the only place he could lie was on the floor which was covered with sharp, broken pieces of brick. Vincent refused to give in. His love of and commitment to Christ could not be shaken. The next ruse to try and break his spirit was to put him in an extra-comfortable bed in the hope that the contrast between that bed and what he had before would weaken his resolve. But that night Vincent died.

It has been written that after St. Vincent died, his body was simply thrown out like a bit of rubbish. Soon vultures came to feast on the body, but then a raven arrived and fought hard to defend the body from the vultures. (This is the reason that one of the "emblems" associated with St. Vincent is a Raven). The story goes on to say that when Governor Dacian heard about this, he ordered that the body be thrown into the sea. This was done, but it was washed up on the shore and a certain widow arranged for the body to be taken and buried outside the walls of Valencia. No doubt she and many others were deeply saddened and moved at what had happened to Vincent and did their utmost to give him a proper burial. When peaceful times came for Christians, a chapel was built over the spot where St. Vincent was buried.

St. Vincent made a name for himself, because the story of his life and heroic martyrdom spread widely. Churches were built in certain countries in Europe, including three in Rome. His name is recorded in one of the writings of St. Augustine, (Sermon 275). He is the most renowned martyr of Spain.

Saint Martin of Tours

St. Martin. What a man! What a saint! What a leader! Although he lived as long ago as the fourth century, (born about 316), we know a great deal about him, unlike many other famous saints or famous people of that era; for few could read or write at that time. We know a good deal about him because someone who got to know him intimately towards the end of his life and who admired him greatly, became determined to write a biography of Martin. Martin was a daring, decisive, unconventional, generous person, whose spur of the moment decisions seemed to always pay off. This person who wrote about him was named Sulpicius Severus. He wrote a detailed biography, travelling back to different parts of Europe in order to speak to many of the people who had been involved in Martin's life.

I already wrote, "What a man! What a saint! What a leader"! Martin did nothing by halves. From what Sulpicius wrote, it is clear that Martin not only did bold, unusual things but was also a very saintly and compassionate person with a strong faith in Christ, who during a long life worked hard to convert the pagans to Jesus Christ, in spite of attacks on his life. And, miraculous cures and happenings were attested to, due to Martin's intervention and his prayers to Heaven.

One famous story that Sulpicius handed down to us is about Martin's pity for a poor, cold beggar whom he encountered and to whom he gave the cloak or mantle he was wearing. This has become famous, because it seemed to catch the imagination of many artists and painters down the centuries and there are many depictions showing Martin, on horseback, handing down his cloak to the poor beggar.

Actually, to be more exact, Sulpicius' story went like this. Martin was a soldier at the time like his father, and only aged 18, and, at the time thinking seriously of converting to Christianity. (As we shall see later in this account, Martin was a reluctant soldier and what he really wanted to become was a Christian monk). He was stationed in Gaul, (now France). It was a cold day when he and other soldiers on horseback and wearing fine uniforms, rode through the gates of the town of Amiens, where there was a poor beggar begging. No one stopped, but when Martin came to him, he was so struck by the sight of a beggar with hardly any clothes on and who looked like he was perishing with the cold, that he stopped. Martin was clad in a coat which was called a cloak or mantle, a large, warm garment without sleeves which you could wrap around yourself. Martin did not waste any time. He took off his cloak, got hold of his sword and cut the cloak down the middle and gave half of it to the beggar and he wrapped the other half around himself.

There is a sequel to the story just told. It was said that Martin had a vivid dream the night after he helped the beggar who was so cold. He dreamt that he was giving his cloak to Jesus Christ, who accepted it. It was after this that Martin took the final step to being baptised a Christian.

Martin was the son of a fairly high-ranking soldier in the Roman Empire, stationed in what is now Hungary. His parents were not Christians, although in later years his mother became one. Martin was attracted to the Christian religion at a fairly young age and started to take instructions. As his father's son, it was customary for him to become a soldier too. He quietly objected and so was given a somewhat pacifist role in the military. Because his father was an officer, Martin became an officer when he joined the military at age 15.

Anyone who has got to know Martin through reading will readily believe this story. As an officer, he was given a servant, a slave, who did the usual chores for Martin. But Martin treated him as another human being. On one occasion, someone, to his amazement, saw Martin cleaning his slave's boots! We do not know what his reason was for doing this, but we know that Martin though unusual, was no fool, so there was no doubt some good reason.

Another story handed down by his biographer goes as follows. Martin was living in Gaul, (Poitiers, France), when he and companions made the trip back to where he lived as a child, (now Hungary), to visit his parents. Going through the Alps, they were attacked and captured by robbers who not only wanted to steal all he had but also threatened their lives. Martin calmly got down to quietly talking to these robbers. It is to be remembered that whoever Martin talked to throughout his life, whether to robbers or pagans or would-be Christians or Roman generals, people could not do other than to stop and listen. He had a riveting personality. Martin and his companions were not harmed. Martin's conversation must have touched on spiritual matters, because one of these robbers was so impressed that he not long after converted and changed his life. Later, the biographer, Sulpicius, made contact with this man. Incidentally, Martin's mother and probably his father too, were later converted to Christianity.

Martin was essentially a man of prayer rather than a soldier. He loved the quiet, prayerful life of a monastery. After he rose to become Abbot of one, he founded two others. Founding a monastery required two things, first the particular area had need of a monastery, and secondly it required someone with enough determination to do the job of starting and building one. His reputation for holiness and teaching spread and attracted many monks to his monasteries, many of them young. He also acquired a reputation for something entirely different--a reputation for having a great compassion for prisoners--for many of them were confined in a jail for unjust reasons and some perhaps were awaiting execution or torture. He would leave the monastery and travel to different places, confront the authorities, who were often generals or important rulers. He was so well-known that these authorities felt they had to listen to his passionate requests. Some of them so feared his arrival that they released the prisoners as soon as they heard he had arrived! No wonder Martin's fame spread!

Martin was also associated with the miraculous cures of serious illnesses and for this reason alone he was in great demand all over Gaul.

In those days, it was usual for the people to choose their bishop. The bishop of Tours died. The people knew that the humble Martin would never agree to leave the monastery outside Tours and become such an important person as a bishop, so they tricked him into coming into Tours from his monastery on some pretext, and when he was in, huge numbers of people who had been hiding suddenly surrounded him. He had to stay! But he insisted on living in a humble abode, not the bishop's usual residence!

So many stories about Martin! He was over 80 when he died. At his request, he was buried in the "Cemetery for the Poor", not in the cemetery that was fitting for a bishop. Not surprising, knowing St. Martin! (See Endnote.)

Endnote.

Incidentally, this fact that St. Martin asked to be buried, not in the main cemetery but in the one for the poor, makes one think of Pope John Paul 11's request that his body, after death, be put into an ultra-poor coffin, not the usual kind of coffin for a pope. The television coverage of the funeral of this saintly pope showed something quite unexpected--this stark, barely-stained coffin.

Saint Nicholas

St. Nicholas lived a long time ago, (he died in 343 A.D.), but his fame when he was alive--his fame for heroic acts of kindness--was such that he has been remembered down the centuries to this day. As many know, he is remembered as "Santa Claus". Of course, now, when we think of Santa Claus, for the sake of children at Christmas time, we invent stories of a person who comes from the North Pole down the chimney and so on.

How did the name Saint Nicholas get changed to Santa Claus? Over the years, St. Nicholas has been remembered and revered in many countries; and somehow, the Dutch words for Saint Nicholas, (Sinter Klaus), has in the English speaking countries been used and slightly changed to Santa Claus.

Nicholas lived in a town called Myra, which is in a country now known as Turkey. His parents died at a fairly young age from a plague which was ravishing the country at the time. He became a priest, and later the bishop of Myra. The money he inherited from his parents he used, over the years, to assist the needy, the sick and the poor.

But his fame, down the centuries, has not come from the fact that he had some surplus money, but from his concern for those in need of any sort. And, often, he would take pains to be generous without letting it be known that he was the benefactor.

There are many stories still written about what Nicholas did. One of them goes as follows. There was a man who had three daughters. He had been fairly comfortably off financially, but for some reason, he lost most of his money. He needed a considerable amount of money to enable his daughters to get married, because in those days it was customary for the father of the bride to offer a dowry to the man, or the family of the man, whom the daughter was hoping to marry. When the eldest daughter was seriously considering marriage, her father found himself in a difficult position. It was then that he found a bag containing some gold coins had been flung into his house one night. Later, when the second daughter was betrothed and he needed a dowry, the same thing happened; some gold coins were mysteriously found in his house. When the time came that the third daughter was being courted, some money arrived again. But, this time, the father somehow found out that the benefactor in each case had been Nicholas.

Sailors of that time had a particular reverence for him. After he died he became a patron saint for sailors. Once, when St. Nicholas was sailing back from a pilgrimage in the Holy Land, the ship ran into such a storm that all seemed to be lost and the sailors were almost in a panic. But the calm Nicholas prayed, and it seemed miraculous that soon after that the storm abated.

Under the Roman Emperor of the time (Diocletian), Christians were severely punished if they persisted in refusing to worship the pagan Roman gods. And so it was that St. Nicholas, at the time he was Bishop of Myra, was put into a jail, together with many other Christians, and suffered horribly there for over five years. He refused to acquiesce to the demands of the Emperor. It was only when Constantine became Emperor that Nicholas was let out of jail.

That St. Nicholas was truly a remarkably saintly person is confirmed by what the world thought of him after he died. As already mentioned, he became a patron saint for sailors, but he later became a patron saint for many other occupations and cities and countries as his popularity spread through the Middle Ages. It has been estimated that more than 2,000 Christian churches were named after him, including four hundred in England, three hundred in Belgium, thirty four in Rome, and twenty three in the Netherlands.

Saint Monica

St. Monica was above all a Mother. She is remembered as an infinitely loving, patient, tireless mother who never gave up her own personal efforts and never gave up storming Heaven with her prayers on behalf of her son. Her son became the great St. Augustine. Monica had three children, and the child of hers who needed her prayers most was her eldest, Augustine, who, after many years of waywardness, became converted, and so strongly converted that he became one of the greatest saints and theologians in the whole history of Christendom.

Monica was born in North Africa of Christian parents in the year 333. Her parents married her at a young age to a much older man, Patricius, who was not a Christian and who had a violent temper. He ridiculed Monica's piety and the efforts she made to be generous to the poor. It is said that Monica was so patient with her husband that, in time, he learned never to use his temper on her. She counselled and urged the various wives that she knew, to be patient with their husbands, because family violence was common. Due to her influence, her husband and his mother later became Christians.

Her son, Augustine, was brilliantly clever, but by his own admission was a "lazy and dissolute youth". He not only abandoned the Christian church, but also abandoned Christian moral standards, lived with a mistress or mistresses and had an illegitimate son.

Monica was a woman of faith and prayer. She attended church daily. She prayed for Augustine and beseeched priests to pray for him. It nearly broke her heart that her son had strayed so far. One priest remarked that Monica had shed so many tears because of her son that it was impossible that he would not change. Actually, the exact wording of that priest that is often quoted is, "It cannot be that the son of those tears should perish".

Augustine moved to Italy, to Rome and then to Milan. Monica followed him later, forever trying to rescue her son from his errors. In Milan, Augustine, in his thirties by then, heard the great Ambrose speak, (Bishop Ambrose, later a saint). He was impressed and had talks with him. Monica also spoke to Ambrose about her son and opened her heart to him. Augustine studied and changed and in time became a convert to Christianity, a very strong one. He wrote endlessly--learned books that are still consulted from the theological viewpoint. His most famous book was his "Confessions", a very long tome and in which, in Book 9 of his work he wrote about his great love for Monica, his mother, and expressed his gratitude for her efforts on his behalf and his admiration for her gifts.

Augustine, in this book, wrote about one of the lengthy conversations he had with his mother, this one was likely the last, for she died not long after. This conversation took place at Ostia, the port for Rome, for he and his mother were waiting for a boat to take them back to North Africa. Augustine took several pages to describe this conversation. He was at the time a fairly new convert to Christianity and rejoiced in it, and Monica was also overjoyed that her son had become such a strong and devoted follower of Christ. The conversation they had dwelt on spiritual matters. Augustine wrote, "......and very sweet was our talk". Finally, Augustine quoted what his mother said to him--touching words--which reflect the beautiful nature that Monica possessed. "My son, as to me, what more I have to do here in this life, and why I am still here, I do not know, since I have no longer anything to hope for in this world. There was only one reason why I wanted to stay a little longer in this life, and that was that I should see you a Christian before I died. Now, God has granted me this beyond my hopes; for, I see that you have despised the pleasures of this world and are becoming His servant. So, what more have I to do here?"

Augustine wrote that about five days after this conversation that his mother lost consciousness for a short while, and when she regained it she said to Augustine and his brother, who was there also, "Where am I?" She was told. Augustine kept quiet and tried to keep back his tears. His brother expressed the hope that she would be buried in her home country (in North Africa). Monica replied, speaking with difficulty "You may lay this body of mine anywhere. Do not worry at all about that. All I ask you is this, that wherever you may be, you will remember me at the altar of the Lord".

Monica died within a few days, in her 56th year. Her task was done. She is a patroness of mothers.

Saint Augustine of Hippo

I have already touched on the life of St. Augustine in the account written about St. Monica, his mother. But, even so, how could I not say more about this great man and saint, who has been described as the most important figure in the ancient Christian Western Church?

As already told, Augustine was born in Tagaste in N. Africa, (now Algeria), in 354 AD. His life as a youth and a young man was ill-spent, as he admitted sorrowfully later. His mother never gave up praying earnestly for his reform. He was enormously talented intellectually. He was offered and accepted the prestigious post of Professor of Rhetoric in Milan, Italy. Here, after a while he came under the influence of the great man and saint, Bishop Ambrose, which moved him in the direction of a conversion to Christianity.

Augustine described his conversion at length in his great book "Confessions", which took many years to complete and is a spiritual autobiography, writing about personal matters, the changes in his spiritual development and his reasons for accepting Christianity with such devotion. This work of his, "Confessions", is of great length, as can be seen by the fact that the description about his conversion to Christianity is in Book V111!

It was when Augustine was about 30 years old, that he was attracted to a conversion. Not only did the teaching and preaching of Bishop Ambrose play a part, but Augustine wrote about other experiences. He was deeply moved after reading the biographical account of how St. Anthony of the Desert, (not to be confused with St. Anthony of Padua), became converted.

St. Anthony, not then a full Christian, wrote that he was perusing through the Christian Gospels when he happened to read the words of Christ, "Go, sell all that you have and give to the poor and you will have treasure in heaven, and come follow me". To St. Anthony, it seemed that what he read was actually spoken to him personally and it had a profound impact on him.

This story of St. Anthony also inspired Augustine, who was in the process of believing in Christ but was hesitating, and, as he said, "fearful of accepting". After reading about St. Anthony, he said to one of his well-read friends, "What are we doing? There are unlearned people taking Heaven by force, while we, with all our knowledge, are so cowardly that we keep rolling around in the mud of our sins". Powerful words!

Augustine described an experience that befell him. It was when he was going through a personal crisis. It seemed that God was begging him to convert, yet he could not summon up enough determination to give up his impure life-style, that he happened to hear a child-like voice coming from the dwelling next door, an arresting voice which kept repeating in this sing-song voice, "Tolle, lege". Translated from the Latin this is, "Take up and read". This had a strong effect on Augustine. He took it that this was nothing else but a command from God to open the book and read "the first page I should find". He picked up the book in front of him which contained the Letters of St. Paul to the Romans and read chapter 13, verses 13 and 14. These are the eloquent words of St. Paul which urge his readers to live a morally pure, sober, peaceful life without envy or greed.

Augustine's life was radically changed. He gave up his teaching position as Professor of Rhetoric. He was baptised a Christian by Bishop Ambrose at Easter time 387. He started to live a simple life without the worldly pleasures he had become accustomed to.

In pondering the factors which contributed to Augustine's conversion one can think of the child-like voice he heard which told him to "Go and read", and one can think of what he learned from the writings of St. Anthony, and the influence of bishop Ambrose; and one cannot forget the unceasing prayers of his saintly mother.

In 387, soon after his mother died, (in Ostia, just outside Rome), he returned to Tagaste in North Africa where he was raised. He lived near the city of Hippo. He lived a sincere, charitable and ascetic Christian life as a monk. On one wall of the room he worked in he had the following written in large letters, "Here we do not speak ill of anyone". It was not long before the Christian people in the area begged him to become a priest, for the bishop, Valerius, was old and dying. Much against the wishes of Augustine he was made a priest. This was in the year 391 and at the age of 36. Then, five years later, at the age of 41, he became bishop of Hippo and was bishop for a long time—a whole 34 years. Augustine took all his various duties as a bishop seriously. Amongst those duties was, of course, that of preaching sermons. Over 500 of those sermons, as taken down by stenographers, have come down to us. He founded three monasteries in Hippo, and near Hippo, a convent for women with his sister, Perpetua, as head. And, in spite of his busy life as a bishop, he continued to find time for contemplation and writing.

His greatest and most widely read book has been "Confessions". In this he examined his relationship with God throughout his life up to the time he stopped writing. He brought into the book many events and experiences and stories of his life. He paid tribute to what his mother did for him. He defended the Christian faith against various heresies. "Confessions" has become a classic of Christian theology and also a classic of world literature. There were also other notable books and hundreds of sermons, letters and papers. It took 11 tomes to fill all his writings! His wise insights and interpretations in the field of Christian theology guided the Church for the next 1,000 years. He is one of the greatest fathers of the Church.

Saint Ambrose

Perusing the biographies of St. Ambrose, it is clear that all those who wrote about him acclaimed him as a remarkable saint who put all his great mental and physical energies to the service of God, whom he loved with all his heart. He has been called Ambrose the Great.

What did he do? A wide variety of things. He was a bishop who as man of action had to wield his authority in a decisive way. He was famous for his spiritual advice and sermons. He is remembered for his writings and music compositions. His noble character was an example to those who came into contact with him. One biographer summarised the life of Ambrose something like this:

"He served as a friend and counsellor to three Roman Emperors. He strove to make the church independent of civil power. He invoked church sanctions against Roman Emperor Theodosius for his massacre of a civilian people. He wrote hymns and wrote books on Scripture, morality, dogma and asceticism."

Ambrose was probably born in 340 and probably in a place called Triers. Triers is in Germany, but in the time of Ambrose, it was said to be in Gaul. Gaul was in the north-western part of the Roman empire. He was the third child of the family. His father was an important Prefect (Roman Empire governor) of Gaul which was a very large province of the Empire. His family were Christian. (As is remembered, Christianity was no longer persecuted after about 312). Ambrose's mother was an especially spiritual person, which can be seen not only in the behaviour of Ambrose but also in her other two children. Marcellina was the eldest child and 10 years older than Ambrose. She later became a nun and made a vow of virginity and she and another young woman who had vowed virginity lived with her mother. Ambrose's brother Satyrus prospered in his political career in the Roman Empire and became a Prefect of a small Roman province. Later, Satyrus voluntarily gave up this position so that he could help Ambrose when he became bishop of Milan, helping in the routine administration of his diocese, so that Ambrose could give his whole attention to other important matters. Ambrose never married. In fact, he had also made a vow of celibacy at quite a young age.

Ambrose's father died in 354, so the family moved back to Rome. Ambrose did well in his studies, and in his religious knowledge and faith. He acquired a mastery of the Greek language which was not common even among the well-educated. He became a lawyer and as the years went by, distinguished himself in the world of law and politics so well that the Roman Emperor of the time heard of him and appointed him as Prefect (Governor) of the northern part of Italy with residence in Milan. It is not known how long he was Prefect here before events occurred to change the direction of his life. But it is known that he earned the love and admiration of his people during that time. He was even accepted by the Arians, a sort of Christian off-shoot, very powerful in and around Milan and a source of serious division among Christians at that time; for their beliefs fell far short of those of orthodox Christians. (More about the Arians later.)

The event which forced Ambrose to change happened in this way. The man who had been bishop of Milan and northern Italy for the previous 20 years was an Arian by belief, having been appointed by a Roman Emperor who had Arian leanings. Not only was this bishop an Arian, which was repugnant to all the orthodox Christians, but he has been described as a tyrant who had a hatred of the Catholics and persecuted them. His name was Auxentius and he had been brought in from the land of Cappadocia, and could not even speak Latin. He had been excommunicated by Pope Damasus, but refused to leave.

In the year 374 Auxentius died. This caused a crisis, because someone had to succeed him as bishop. Was it to be another Arian or a Catholic? The Roman Emperor of the time, Valentinian , decided that there had to be an election. Expecting this election to be fiery, Ambrose, as the Prefect of that area, decided he had to attend the election in an attempt to mediate and keep peace. Although Ambrose was primarily a governor, yet, he had taken a keen, heart-felt and co-operative interest in religious affairs.

Who were the Arians? The Arians in different parts of the empire in that 4th century A.D. became quite powerful rivals to Catholics and orthodox Christians. This was in spite of the fact that at the famous Christian meeting, the Council of Nicea, in the year 325, (See Endnotes), it had already been passed that the beliefs of the Arians were heretical and invalid. Believers in Arianism, in its full form, did not believe in the Holy Trinity, nor in the divinity of Christ--the belief that Jesus was the son of God the Father. This was, of course, a radical departure from what was regarded as the truth to the orthodox Christians and it is no wonder that St. Ambrose and many other Christian leaders, (St. Athanasius and St. Hilary being notable ones), struggled so hard to overcome the Arian heresy.

Returning to the events of 374, when an election was held to determine who was to be the next bishop of Milan and what is now northern Italy, it has already been mentioned that Prefect Ambrose felt, for the sake of peace, that he had to take a part in this election, with clergy and citizens present. He opened the meeting speaking in a calm, conciliatory manner. Then, an astounding thing happened. His speech was suddenly interrupted by a voice, crying out, "Ambrose, Bishop". This same cry, "Ambrose, Bishop", was immediately loudly repeated by seemingly the whole assembly, showing how highly he was regarded as a man and a leader. Ambrose, one feels sure, was the kind of person, who, by simply looking at him and hearing him speak, immediately inspired confidence, such was his intelligence, obvious integrity and commanding presence.

The meeting was over. It was clear that the majority were strongly in favour of Ambrose being the next bishop, even though he was a politician rather than a church man. It has to be remembered that, in that age, it was not unheard of for someone who was just a humble monk to be swept in as pope; or for someone not even in the clergy to be acclaimed a bishop.

But, the story is not quite over. With this sudden, extraordinary turn of events, Ambrose was far from happy. He fled to a friend's house to think things over and could not be found for a while. In spite of the overwhelming confidence the assembly at the election had placed in him, he was reluctant to accept. Then came the letter from the Roman Emperor, who had been keeping a close interest in the election, in which he wrote, "I know of no bishop worthy of the name, except Ambrose". Ambrose came out of hiding and accepted.

Ambrose, therefore, found himself the new bishop of Milan. With his upbringing and study, he was already a strong Christian. Certainly, his numerous writings on a wide variety of Christian topics during his life attest to his devotion to Christ and his deep ecclesiastical knowledge from an early age. He had a particular devotion to the writings of St. Basil. He corresponded with St. Basil.

But, in spite of this background of learning, when he became Bishop of Milan, he wasted no time before he made another careful study of the Scriptures. He also divested himself of his worldly goods. His personal property he gave to the poor. Any lands he gave to the Church. He made provision for his beloved sister, Marcellina, a nun, who had been living with her mother while she was alive. Marcellina lived a particularly Christian life and was later called a saint; it is not clear if she was officially canonised or whether she was simply seen as being saintly. His brother Satyrus came to help him with the running of the diocese and Satyrus was also of assistance to their sister. One cannot help but admire this family of St. Ambrose.

Ambrose lived a simple, ascetic life. He ate sparingly, only having a proper dinner on a Saturday or a Sunday or on a festival day of a well-known martyr. He spent a good deal of his nights in prayer or writing down important thoughts that had come into his mind or replying to the large amount of correspondence that came to him. The amount of work he was able to get through was prodigious. He found time to write many important books.

He was an extraordinarily talented speaker and devoted much care and energy to his talks and homilies. Every Sunday he spoke at the Basilica and this drew huge crowds and he converted many, (including St. Augustine of Hippo and many who had been Arians). It is said that the influence of St. Ambrose was so wide and strong that, after a time there were not many Arians left in and around Milan. He did not read his homilies from what he had already prepared, but "spoke from his heart". His love of and knowledge of the Scriptures inspired his preaching. With his untiring efforts and his kindness, especially to the poor he grew to be a beloved bishop of Milan.

The Roman Emperors of the time often chose to seek the advice of Ambrose of Milan, because of his reputation for wisdom and sound judgement. And he used his energies to combat heresies such as the Arian beliefs and to combat attempts to return to the worship of paganism. He found himself in the position of having to strongly resist the attempts of the Arians to take over the Church.

In the year 386 the Roman Emperor of the time, the youthful Valentinian 11, (the son of Valentinian1), and his mother, Justina, (who wielded a great deal of power), both having become Arians, demanded that Bishop Ambrose give up two churches in Milan for use by Arians. Ambrose refused. He was then required to answer for his actions at a council. At this council of clergy, Ambrose's eloquent defence of the orthodox Christian church as opposed to the heretical Arian belief, was so strong that the meeting ended without him having to make any surrender of these churches to the Arians.

However, the young Emperor Valentinian and his mother were not finished. Ignoring Bishop Ambrose, they gave orders that preparations should be made for themselves and their retinue to use one of these Milan churches for a service on a certain day. Ambrose's written reply of refusal, (still extant), is a classic. (See Endnotes). When the Emperor and his mother and retinue arrived, Ambrose and the church congregation were occupying the church. They thought better than to proceed any further and left.

It is of interest that, at a later time, after his mother had died, Emperor Valentinian 11 became a sincere follower of Ambrose and gave up his Arian adherence. Indeed, Arianism gradually faded. (See Endnotes).

Ambrose decided he had to intervene when Theodosius was the Roman Emperor. At a time when Emperor Theodosius was in the East, in Thessalonica, (in modern day Greece), rioters, unhappy with the Roman Prefect of the time, attacked the stronghold of the Prefect, and he was killed. When Emperor Theodosius heard about this he ordered a punishment of the rioters. This punishment resulted in a tragedy. Thousands of innocent Thessalonians were massacred. The world was shocked on hearing this. Theodosius had hitherto won a reputation for being a benign ruler. This was considered "out of character" for him. Ambrose already knew the Emperor and was on good terms with him and was especially shocked.

Ambrose felt compelled to write a letter to the Emperor about what he had done. He told him that he, the Emperor, was denied the Eucharist in church, (excommunication), until he had done penance. He exhorted Emperor Theodosius to undergo a sincere penance and he asked him to remember and imitate King David of old, who repented humbly and publically on a famous occasion.

Theodosius was evidently truly penitent. He submitted to the decision of Ambrose. Ambrose released him from his penance several months later. Theodosius's penance was certainly sincere and not concealed from the public. He and Ambrose became close.

Ambrose officiated at Emperor Theodosius's funeral a few years later, (395). At his funeral, Ambrose spoke to all and described the penance that Theodosius chose to undergo after the massacre at Thessalonica. Ambrose had obviously been touched by the sincerity of his penance. In Ambrose's oration he said that Emperor Theodosius had, "stripped himself of every emblem of royalty, and he publically, in church, bewailed his sin. Nor was there afterwards a day on which he did not grieve for his mistake".

Ambrose was present at Emperor Theodosius' bedside before his death. Ambrose's name was constantly on Theodosius's lips. Ambrose described what Theodosius said in his final minutes. He expressed more concern about the churches in his empire than on his impending death. Later, after he died, Ambrose wrote, "I loved him and am confident that the Lord will listen to the prayer I send up for his pious soul". Only two years later Ambrose died.

As one biographer wrote, "Only two years elapsed before a kindly death reunited two magnanimous souls".

As can be seen, there had grown a deep respect and love between Ambrose, the Bishop of Milan and the Roman Emperor Theodosius.

St Ambrose died on Good Friday, April 4, 397. The following day, there was such an outpouring of emotion that five bishops had difficulty in keeping up with the crowds who kept coming to the basilica in Milan for Christian baptism.

One can see that St. Ambrose was an outstanding bishop and church leader, extraordinarily energetic, wise, courageous and warm. Also, he left posterity a large amount of his writings. This reflects his mental energies and his deep spirituality. All his writings were compiled and printed in Rome in 1580, in five volumes. Some of these are of the many greatly admired sermons he preached, which were put into writing by those who heard him speak. There are other writings of his on a wide variety of spiritual matters. Some of the topics he wrote on were, Eucharist (true body of Christ), the Holy Spirit, advice on prayer, Jesus Christ's suffering in the Passion, the Blessed Virgin Mary, Mary's Visitation to Elizabeth, St. Thomas the apostle, (Doubting Thomas). One biographer of Ambrose compiled no less than 45 notable quotations from his writings or sermons, some of which are in Endnote 4.

St. Augustine of Hippo once expressed the opinion that of all the spiritual writers he had read, the two who had the most influence on him were St. Augustine and St. Ambrose. (Of course, as you will no doubt remember, St.

Augustine not only read works of St. Ambrose, but also listened to his sermons when he was in Milan.)

Even though it is over 1600 years since the time of St. Ambrose, it seems to me that one cannot help but be touched by the story of this man.

Endnotes.

1. It was at the Council of Nicea (325) that the Nicene Creed was formulated. It has been augmented since then. It is still said in Christian churches, but not as commonly as the Apostle's Creed, which was formulated before it.
2. A portion of this letter of St. Ambrose to the Roman Emperor Valentinian 11, in which he refused to allow a church in Milan to be used for an Arian church service is as follows:

   "If you demand my person, I am ready to submit; you can carry me to prison or to death, I will not resist. But, I will never betray the church of Christ. I will die at the foot of the altar rather than desert it".

3. Arianism did not fade away completely. There are still some Arian believers in the world today.
4. Three of the famous 45 Quotations of St. Ambrose still extant:

   "I will glory not because I am righteous but because I have been redeemed by Christ. I will glory not because I am free from sins but because my sins are forgiven me. I will not glory because I have done good nor because someone has done good to me, but because Christ is my advocate with the Father and because the blood of Christ has been shed for me".

"God knows the future with as much certainty as He knows the present".

"St. Thomas, (*Doubting Thomas, the apostle),* had reason to be amazed when he saw the risen Christ come in unhindered through doors which were barred, (since all the doors were closed). Christ penetrated closed doors, not by his incorporeal nature, but with the quality of his resurrection".

Saint Jerome

Not only was St. Jerome a great saint, but he was a famous historical person because he "translated the Bible". He was a scholarly man who early in life mastered the Latin and Greek languages, and later in life mastered Hebrew, so that he translated most of the books of the Bible, that is he translated both the texts written in Greek and in Hebrew into Latin, the common language of the day. This translation is known as the Vulgate. This took a good deal of his life.

Jerome was born in about 347 A.D., in an area which is in today's world, close to the border of Italy and Slovenia. His parents were Christian and he was brought up as such. It is to be noted that 347 A.D., when he was born, was after the Roman Emperor Constantine lifted the persecutions of Christians in the Roman Empire.

Jerome must have shown intellectual promise, because his parents sent him to Rome for study, and, particularly to study Latin and Greek. He had a natural gift for languages and it was not long before he became fluent in these languages.

But, the company he kept in Rome drew him away from his faith and he lived a somewhat licentious life. A little later, when he came to his senses, his remorse for how he had spent his time struck him with extreme sorrow and shame.

Jerome was not just proficient in learning different languages, but he was also a powerful speaker. In those days oratory was one of the skills commonly taught in places of learning and Jerome took advantage of this. Actually, later in life, because of his natural talents and his training, he became a redoubtable opponent in debate, especially when the Christian faith was threatened. Some opponents, ruefully or even angrily, described him as a person who possessed a very sharp tongue!

At the time when he was beginning to feel truly sorry for his sins, it is said that Jerome had a vision or dream—of Jesus Christ himself. This led him to ask himself what course he was going to take in life. Was he going to reform in a small way or wholly?

Jerome must have said a whole-hearted "Yes" to the reform in his life he felt he was being asked for. For, he changed his life around radically, right until he died. He lived an ascetic life, renounced the worldly pleasures he was used to. He traveled to a part of Syria which was partly a desert, and where many others of the same persuasion went to do penance at that time. He spent a whole four years there, studying, praying and fasting and also learning the Hebrew language, mostly from a Jewish scholar.

It is worth quoting, (from one of his letters to a friend), what Jerome wrote about during his time of penance in Syria. During that time his health was poor and he was beset with strong temptations. One notes not only his sincerity but also his eloquence. And also, one notes his long sentences!

> "In the remotest part of a wild and stony desert, burnt up with the heat of the sun, so scorching that it even frightens the monks who live there, I seemed myself to be in the midst of the delights of Rome…..in this exile and prison to which, through Hell, I had voluntarily condemned myself, with no other company than scorpions and wild beasts, many times I imagined myself watching the dancing maidens, as if I had been in the midst of them. My face was pallid with fasting, yet my will felt the attacks of desire…….. passion was still alive. Alone with the enemy, I threw myself, in spirit at the feet of Jesus, watering them with my tears and tamed my flesh by fasting for whole weeks. I am not ashamed to disclose my temptations, though I grieve I am not now what I was then".

Jerome returned to Rome. The pope of the time, Pope Damasus, got to know him, and, in fact, Jerome became one of his important advisors. The pope asked him to change and revise the current Greek version of the New Testament, which seemed to have many errors. Jerome did this and also completed some other Bible revisions. The pope started him off on the main work of his life, the translation of the Bible.

At that time, in Rome, Jerome started a new movement of Christian asceticism, which influenced many people, especially a number of well-born, pious women, some of them later to be canonized saints. One of these women who Jerome worked with for the rest of his life was Paula, later St. Paula. She, being well-off, helped him later financially, allowing him to devote the latter part of his life to translating the Scriptures commissioned by the pope, and to perform other writings.

Jerome tended to be passionate in his likes and dislikes. He got himself disliked by some because of his blunt attacks on what he felt was obvious wrong-doing and hypocrisy. Even a few members of the Christian clergy, who were not living up to their calling, were not spared.

St. Jerome's remaining years were spent in the Holy Land, in fact in Bethlehem. He lived and wrote in a cave not far from the birthplace of Jesus. With the financial help of Paula he spear-headed the building of monasteries in and around Bethlehem. Paula became head of one of these monasteries for women. There were numerous pilgrims to Bethlehem from many lands and a hospice was built for these pilgrims and other travelers.

But the main work for Jerome, which he was wholly dedicated to during those latter days, was the translations of the Scriptures, the translation of the Hebrew and Greek texts into Latin. It has been said that he was adept at clarifying difficult passages. The only parts of the Latin Bible which were not translated nor worked over by him were the Books of Wisdom, Ecclesiasticus, Baruch and the two Books of Maccabees 3. He wrote on other Christian matters as well and left three volumes of letters. (See Endnote).

Jerome left a wonderful description of what life was like, all around him in Bethlehem, a peaceful, harmonious life among people from all countries.

"Illustrious people from Gaul congregate here, and no sooner has a Briton converted to religion than he leaves his land of the early-setting sun to seek a land which he only knows by reputation and from the Scriptures. Then, the Armenians, the Persians, the peoples of India and Ethiopia, of Egypt, Pontus, Cappadocia, Syria and Mesopotamia! They come in throngs and set us examples of every virtue. The languages are different but the religion is the same. As many different choirs chant the psalms as there are nations".

St. Jerome died in Bethlehem in 420. The famous Council of Trent (1545-1563) declared Jerome's "Vulgate" Scripture translation an official text of the Catholic Church. It has been written that Jerome's accomplishments in biblical studies are without parallel in Christian history. But, one is impressed that in his other writings, he shows how humble he was and how open he was about his weaknesses.

Endnote.

The "New American Bible" (1970) is widely read. Like St. Jerome's work it was a translation from the original languages, not just a revision of a book already written. And it took 50 scholars 25 years to complete it! This tells us something about the magnificence of St. Jerome's work.

Saint Patrick

St. Patrick, the great apostle of Ireland, lived a colourful and heroic life. At a comparatively young age, at a time of personal suffering, his faith and piety grew strong and this led to the conviction that he should strive to evangelise Ireland.

What we know about his life derives partly from stories handed down through the centuries (tradition) and partly from two accounts written by himself, (one of these being his "Confessio" or memoirs), from biographies written from the 7ᵗʰ centuries on, and here and there from historical documents.

It is perhaps strange that there is uncertainty as to whether he was born in South Wales, or whether he was born near Dumbarton, close to the west coast of Scotland. He was born in or around A.D. 387, born of Christian parents. His father worked in an official position for the Roman Emperor in different parts of the Roman Empire. (See Endnotes). There is something to be said in favour of the latter place, Dumbarton, being his birth place rather than South Wales, because we do know that at the age of

16, he and others were captured by pirates from Ireland and taken across the sea to the northern part of Ireland where he languished as a slave, labouring on the land. And, this part of Ireland is quite a short distance from the Dumbarton part of Scotland, but a long way from South Wales.

As I said earlier, Patrick's faith flourished at this time of personal suffering. One can imagine what he went through, being dragged away from his parents and home at the age of 16, and off to a foreign country to become a slave. During the six years he was there, his prayer-life became stronger, and it seems that at the end of those years he received some kind of heavenly message to run away. So, this he did and he had to trudge many miles to a port on the coast of Ireland, where he managed to get on a boat about to cross the sea. He got to see his parents and home again.

By this time he had resolved to give his life to God as a religious person. He travelled over to what is now France, spent time at St. Martin's monastery in Tours, which was famous at the time for learning and piety. He became ordained as a priest and worked for a time in this part of Europe. But, his thoughts were turning more and more to Ireland. Patrick wrote in his "Confessio", (his memoirs), that he had a vision a few years after leaving Ireland. In this vision, a man gave him a letter, entitled "The Voice of the Irish", and as Patrick read this letter it seemed to him that the people he had known when he was in Ireland were earnestly begging him to return. He felt he should heed this sincere request. However, to return to Ireland to undertake the arduous task of converting the people from paganism, (Druidism), to Christianity was enough to fill anyone with dread. But, it did not stop Patrick.

It appears that Patrick showed strong leadership qualities from a young age. The pope of the time, Pope Celestine 1, entrusted Patrick with this mission of conversion and so Patrick and some helpers set off for Ireland.

As soon as Patrick and his followers arrived in Ireland they were attacked by the pagan Druids, who did not want their religion replaced by another one. Through a great deal of Patrick's life in Ireland until he died, he had to contend with this strong opposition from the Druids and other enemies of Christianity. He wrote in his "Confessio" that many times he and his companions were seized and carried off as captives, and on one occasion he was loaded with chains and the decision was made that he should be killed. He was a man of prayer, penance and self denial. Heaven helped him. He escaped.

Also, initially, he had opposition from some of the Irish kings and chieftains. There is a story that, at one time, he got out of a boat in Strangford Lough (in Ulster), wanting to continue his journey on foot when he was approached by an angry chieftain, named Dichu who drew his sword and was about to strike Patrick when it seemed that the chieftain's arm suddenly got stuck and "stiff as a statue", as though the arm had become paralysed.

The people of Ireland were won over by Patrick's faith, courage and meekness--without any pretence of superiority; and also by miracles that seemed to accompany him; and also, of course, by the story of Christ. Some of those who were converted most strongly were sons and daughters of the kings and chieftains. Patrick himself wrote that he converted "many thousands" to the faith. Many converts became devout Christians, to the extent of being called saints. As time went on, he ordained priests and made bishops. He travelled, (and no doubt he had many helpers and companions), over a good deal of Ireland, particularly in the north and the west. He never rested. He came to be known as the one who "found Ireland all heathen and left it all Christian".

The people of Ireland were certainly not averse to hearing the stories of Jesus Christ, about his miracles and his teaching. Just the opposite. They were ready for conversion. We have nearly all heard that Patrick made use of the Irish shamrock to try and explain the Blessed Trinity-- three leaves coming from the one stem.

There is no doubt that Patrick was successful in his mission to bring Ireland to Christianity. And, there is no doubt that Patrick was a man of prayer. This practical success went hand in hand with his prayer life. From time to time, it is said, that he "withdrew from the world". One of the places he went to was the small island on Lough Derg, and it is a fact that this is still a place that people go to for a spiritual retreat. (See Endnotes).

Then, one cannot leave without mentioning Croagh Patrick, (St. Patrick's mountain). This is a mountain in County Mayo, on the west coast of Ireland, looking out on to the Atlantic. It is said that St. Patrick liked to spend time on this mountain, taking shelter in a cave if necessary, for the purpose of prayer and penance. It is said that he once spent 40 days on or around this mountain for this purpose. (See Endnotes).

St. Patrick died in the land that he evangelised. It was on March 17th and the year was probably 493. He died in a little place called Saul, close to Downpatrick in Northern Ireland, and it is said that his remains were buried in the local chieftain's fort, where later there was built the cathedral of Down in Downpatrick.

Endnotes

1. Roman Emperor Constantine, having won the battle of Milvian Bridge in 312 A.D., during which battle, according to legend, he saw a vision of the Christian cross, he made an order that from then on Christianity would no longer be persecuted, but tolerated. So, one can understand that at the time when Patrick was born, (c 387), Christians were free to practice their faith.

2. (Personal). My dear Irish wife, when she was a teenager, and again a few years later, went for a weekend retreat of prayer and penance to this Lough Derg, known unofficially as St. Patrick's Purgatory. Of course she did not go alone, but went in a group. She is fond of describing the rigours, (and laughs about it), for instance the scanty and basic food and the hard benches to sleep on!

3. (Personal). Being that my wife was born and brought up in County Mayo, near Croagh Patrick Mountain, I have therefore visited this part of Ireland on many occasions. I remember one day when I was there during one of the summer months, and when the annual pilgrimage to the top of this mountain took place, (a Sunday). On that day hundreds of people climb up to the tiny chapel at the summit of the mountain. I have myself climbed this mountain more than once with gratifying results, because, for one thing, it is scenically very beautiful.

Saint Brendan

The next three saints I am writing about are St. Brendan, St. Columba and St. Aidan. All three were Irish saints who lived about the same time, that is approximately in the 500's and 600's A.D., not long after Ireland was converted to Christianity. St. Patrick died probably in 493. Something else these three saints had in common is that they did not confine their work to Ireland, but laboured elsewhere. They were "overseas missionaries"!

Actually, in the wake of St. Patrick's work of conversion there was a surge of culture and of missionary work among Irish men and women. Their efforts extended beyond Ireland and many Irish monks worked wonders in Scotland, northern England and even in Europe. Monasteries did not just seek to preach and instruct in Christianity, but gradually became centres of learning and of charitable works. (See Endnote). Perhaps it was this that gave origin to the saying, "Ireland, the land of saints and scholars".

This name Brendan has come down through the centuries and many Irishmen have been given this name.

(Yes. It is worth being named after a saint especially if one's parents remind their sons and daughters why they were so named.)

St. Brendan was born in 484 A.D. in south west Ireland, not far from where Tralee now stands. He accomplished much in Ireland, preaching Christianity. He became a monk and then a priest and then an abbot. It was not an easy life, the life of a monk. Monks had to adhere to a rigorous life-style and many were brought up as monks and learnt self-discipline from an early age. Their day, busy with work and prayer, started very early and they were rightfully ready for rest when it came to bed time. Brendan was one of the many from Ireland who travelled outside their country to teach and evangelise, using monasteries as their centres of activity. Brendan founded many monasteries. The most famous one was at Clonfert, (County Galway in Ireland). His missionary zeal took him to Scotland, particularly to the famous monastery of Iona, started and founded by St. Columba, (originally from Ireland), and to Wales and England. He was for three years in Britain. Like many saints he had abundant faith and energy and also, in common with other saints, he did not seem to show any fear in situations and facing decisions where most people would have cringed.

St. Brendan is particularly well-known for his voyage into the Atlantic, the book that described it being the "Navigatio Brendani", written in Latin. He did this in his old age by which time he was greatly loved and revered by all, and many monks were ready to follow him. Some think that he may have crossed the Atlantic. They were away seven years apparently, so they could have gone a long way and spent considerable time in foreign lands in that time. It appears that Brendan and his fellow monks came back with fruits and precious stones not before seen in Ireland.

Much has been written and in different languages about Brendan's voyage. The book, the "Navigatio Brendani", (often shortened to just "Navigatio",) was not written by St. Brendan but was written several centuries later, compiled from what Brendan and his monks must have reported after their return. Some scholars have suggested that it was written about 800 AD and others have put it a century or two after this.

This story of Brendan's voyage has certainly caught the imagination of people ever since. Whereas some have shown evidence that Brendan could well have crossed the Atlantic, others have been almost incredulous that anyone could have done this in the sixth century, that is two or three centuries before the Vikings, (the Norsemen), and about ten centuries before Columbus. In connection with Christopher Columbus, it is interesting to note that clearly the story of Brendan's voyage became well-known and respected widely, for it is on record that Columbus, on one of his travels to the West Indies, made an attempt to find "St. Brendan's Island".

From the maritime and nautical viewpoint it can be shown that it was not impossible for St. Brendan and his monks to have crossed to North America. In the days of Brendan, Irish mariners had been in the forefront of oceanic seafaring. They had built their efficient curraghs (boats) and were experienced in using them, not just around Ireland but up the west coast of Scotland, to the Hebrides, the Orkney Islands, the Faroe Islands, and

Norse sagas report that the Irish were in Iceland before they were.

What is of great interest and what helps sustain the claim that seamen and the curraghs of those times could have crossed the Atlantic is the fact that Englishman Tim Severin set out to see if he could do this, using exactly the same type of boat (curragh) as St. Brendan did. Tim Severin set off with a few men as crew in a replica of a curragh in 1976, along the route considered the most likely to have been used by St. Brendan, (the "Stepping Stones Route"), and he reached Newfoundland! More of this and of St. Brendan's voyage according to the "Navigatio" later.

St. Brendan had a very full life before he embarked on his famous voyage which he did in his seventies. A certain prophesy was made towards the end of his voyage that he would not live long after he returned. He was welcomed back home to his monastery and indeed died shortly after.

Endnote.

Yes, besides teaching and preaching, monasteries were also centres of learning and craftmanship. A good example of this is the world-famous "Book of Kells". The book contains the four Gospels of the New Testament, (of St. Jerome's Vulgate translation of the Bible). It was artistically crafted and finished, (written in Latin), around 800 AD. How many years it took to produce we do not know. It was possibly begun in the Iona monastery in the west of Scotland and then transferred to Kells monastery in Ireland where it remained and survived some violence.

The monastery was plundered by the Vikings but the book was spared, and on another occasion it was stolen and recovered, (partly torn).It is now housed in Dublin's Trinity College.

This four volume book is wonderfully illustrated ("illuminated"). The intricate artistry of almost every letter of almost every word, (in different colours), is such a source of wonder and admiration that the book has in the past been described as "the work of angels"!

Appendix to "Saint Brendan"

Saint Brendan's Voyage and
the Voyage of the "Brendan"

As I, the writer, have already mentioned, St. Brendan ventured out from Ireland into the Atlantic, probably in about 530. And Tim Severin crossed the Atlantic in exactly the same type of boat, named the "Brendan" in 1976, that is about 1,500 years later. In this writing, I will describe the main experiences of those engaged in these two voyages.

St. Brendan undertook this famous voyage into the Atlantic and he and his fellow monks were away for seven years. They could have gone a long way in that time, even taking into consideration that bad winds could have blown them back at times and also that they probably spent their winters on land, that is on some island. They came back with some fruits and precious stones, not usually seen in Ireland. Brendan set off for his voyage when he was quite old and by that time he had acquired fame for many holy accomplishments. He was greatly loved by his monks and they would follow him anywhere.

Sometime before Brendan decided on taking this voyage, it has been described that Brendan was approached by a monk named Barind who told him that he and another monk had come back from a voyage they had taken, and they had eventually found a land so wondrous that they called it "The Promised Land of the Saints". Barind strongly urged Brendan to search for this land for himself. The description of Barind was such that Brendan decided to set off on this voyage, which he and his monks regarded as a holy mission.

St. Brendan's voyage and wanderings were written about in the "Navigatio Brendani", a book written in Latin a few centuries after St. Brendan lived. He and his monks sailed in a "curragh", the very efficient boat which Irish mariners had had a great deal of experience with. These mariners were accustomed to travel not just around Ireland but a long way beyond. These curraghs were open, flat-bottomed boats, (but often partly covered by some sort of canvas covering), and oars were used together with probably one mast and a sail. They were constructed with great care, were made of a wooden frame, covered by ox-hides, sewn on, after having been well tanned with oak bark and then this "leather" was smeared with wool fat. It is probable that St.Brendan went with about 15 monks. We do not know the size of the curragh they went in or whether there was more than one curragh. No doubt rowing was needed when there was no helpful wind for sailing, so they certainly needed many men to take turns at rowing. In the "Navigatio" book it was written that the monks took extra ox hide with them.

It is likely that they took the well-known "Stepping Stones Route", the usual route at that time for travelling into the Atlantic, and used by Irish Christian monks to make settlements on the islands on that route. And also, descriptions in the "Navigatio" fit in to what would probably have been encountered by Brendan and his men on this particular route. This route comprised Ireland, the west coast of Scotland, the Hebrides, the Faroe islands and Norse (Viking) sagas strongly suggest that the Irish were in Iceland, even before they, the Norsemen were. In other words, this route that they took went far north and then far west.

I have already said that Tim Severin and helpers built a boat, which he named the "Brendan", built as close a replica to the curragh of St. Brendan as it was possible to build, in which to try and cross the Atlantic. Severin had read the book "Navigatio", in fact he had studied it with care and was intrigued by it. He was pretty sure that St. Brendan must have reached Iceland, but could not tell for certain from the study of the book whether or not he completed the crossing of the Atlantic. Tim Severin was determined to try and make the crossing in a curragh, and he made it. After it was all over, Severin wrote a book and also made a film about his successful voyage in the "Brendan" from Ireland to Newfoundland. The book is titled "The Brendan Voyage" and won many prestigious awards. Tim Severin, an Englishman, is a graduate (Honours) of Oxford University.

It took Tim Severin nearly three years of meticulous research, planning and building before his boat was completed. It was built in a noted boat-yard in Co. Cork, Ireland, launched with pomp and ceremony by

Tim's daughter, having been blessed, (and incorporating a special poem composed for the occasion), by Bishop Casey. It was, of course, an open boat but tent-like canvas was spread over part of the boat. It had two masts with two square sails with large images of the Celtic cross on each sail. The wood lattice-type frame was made of Irish ash and this was covered with exactly the same "leather" as the original curraghs-- ox-hide, tanned with oak bark and then smeared with wool fat.

Tim Severin spent time in the Irish National Museum in Dublin to research much of the curragh-making techniques of old and with respect to the types of metal (iron) needles that were used to stitch the hides together. He wrote, "What exquisite skills they had in Brendan's day".

Tim Severin and five crew set off from Brandon's Creek in S.W. Ireland on May 16th 1976. He chose the most likely route that St. Brendan would have taken, namely the Stepping Stones route. They travelled north towards the Hebrides and after several adventures, storms and near-disasters, arrived in Iona, an island on the west coast of Scotland. Here they went ashore and were greeted and invited to lunch by the Abbot at the Benedictine monastery of Iona. This monastery had been restored, (having been destroyed on more than one occasion by those war-like Vikings of the distant past). Iona had been a very busy monastery in the time of St. Brendan. It had been founded by St. Columba. St. Brendan had been to Iona before, (obviously in a curragh, and maybe more than once), before he took his final voyage, and had, no doubt, met St. Columba.

Tim Severin on the "Brendan" reached the Faroe islands, north- west of Scotland, on June 24th, 1976. One of the many islands of the Faroes is called the "Isle of the Sheep" where they found a large number of very large white sheep. Also, in the "Navigatio", (chapter 9), it is described how St. Brendan and his monks went ashore on an island where there were an extraordinary number of large sheep. The book says, "Sheep so numerous that they hid the face of the land". Scholars have shown how closely the "Navigatio" description of this island fits what is now known as the "Isle of the Sheep".

Tim Severin and his crew spent time in the Faroe islands, met many people, including one young man who had been on the sea since a child and who asked to join the crew of the "Brendan". He was taken on. Severin wrote in his book, "Saint Brendan's name is familiar to every citizen of the Faroes, who learns in school that the Irish priests were the first people to settle in their remote islands".

While St. Brendan was on this island of the sheep, where the "Navigatio" says they were from Holy Thursday to Holy Saturday, they met one of the islanders who brought them food and predicted that they would be on another island just after Easter, called the Paradise of Birds. In chapter 11 of the "Navigatio" it is written that the monks found a huge tree with a multitude of white birds on this island. The monks stayed on this island until "the eighth day of Pentecost". (From Easter to Pentecost is about 50 days).

In his book, The "Voyage of the Brendan", Severin also describes huge numbers of birds. They were sailing by one of the Sheep islands and saw. "Thousands and thousands of seabirds pouring out of the cliffs – gulls, guillemots, razorbills, fulmars, gannets, puffins, skuas and terns".

Incidentally, it is worthy of comment that, reading the "Navigatio", it is noted that St. Brendan and his monks, all through their voyage, lasting seven years, were scrupulously faithful to their religious ritual, with their daily prayers and masses and they did not neglect to pay respect to the liturgical times of the year, that is Easter, Christmas, Epiphany, Lent etc. I, the author, think it is not too far-fetched to suggest that the monks may well have kept up their laborious rowing to the accompaniment of singing or chanting or praying in chorus! Others have done something similar, and the work is made easier.

After leaving the Sheep islands, St. Brendan and his men were utterly exhausted after three months on the sea with unfavourable winds, when they sighted an island on Christmas Day and went ashore. They were met by an elderly man who took them to a community which had a monastery and a church. They were warmly greeted and well-looked after. The Abbot himself washed their feet and they were fed and given accommodation. The "Navigatio" describes how food seemed to miraculously arrive and lamps seemed to miraculously never go out!

Tim Severin and crew had the companionship of whales, (small and huge), dolphins and seals, especially travelling from the Faroes to Iceland. Not only dolphins but small whales enjoyed swimming right under their boat. The "Brendan" had reference books to read up about whales and the birds they encountered, and also the Faroe islander they had with them, Trondor by name, was a gold-mine of information, not only about sailing in those waters, but also about marine life. They saw one whale, the only whale which Trondor was seriously afraid of and which he called a "spaekhugger". It was a "killer whale" Tim Severin wrote. They were all relieved when this whale swam near and then decided to swim away again.

St. Brendan and his monks, as described in the "Navigatio", encountered and were amazed and alarmed at the "sea beasts", some of them "spouting foam from their nostrils". They did not know that such large creatures existed. (Obviously, these were whales.) They saw the shocking sight of two sea monsters fighting and the death of one of them. The monks were very fearful at the sight of this, but Brendan comforted them.

As I shall discuss later, most of the tale, "Navigatio", written a long time after St. Brendan lived, sounds realistic but part of the tale sounds to us fanciful, as though perhaps a folk-lore had grown up around the original story between the time of the actual voyage and the time "Navigatio' was written. Some of the descriptions of "sea beasts" used by the author certainly seem like what we know as whales. But then others are difficult to understand. It was written that St. Brendan encountered a particularly huge "sea monster" and it was given the name of Jascon. It came alongside their curragh and stayed for a while. Some monks thinking it was an island went on to it and started to light a fire on its back!

Both St. Brendan in his curragh and Tim Severin in his "Brendan" had difficulty in sailing against the wind with the somewhat primitive sailing methods of their boats. They both found themselves being blown back or around in a circle at times. They were both very dependent on the right direction of the wind. It seems from the narrative that St. Brendan and the curragh were blown a long way back to the Sheep Islands more than once.

When the "Brendan" approached Iceland from the south, Tim Severin was on the lookout for volcanoes, because research had shown him that the southern tip of Iceland and the islands off the shore were noted for erupting volcanoes, and also that the volcanoes had probably been more active in previous centuries.

The "Navigatio" told of fearful experiences in the latter part of St. Brendan's voyage, (Chapter 23). The monks saw what seemed like a "smith's forge", with loud noises, fire, heat and lumps coming down from the top of the hill on the island and running into the sea, where they seemed to make the water boil. Most scholars agree that the "Navigatio" was describing the eruption of a volcano in Iceland or in one of the islands off Iceland. Iceland being notorious for its volcanoes, this description lends credibility to the claim that St. Brendan, at least, reached Iceland.

The crew of the "Brendan" went ashore in Reyjkavic, Iceland on July 15th 1976. They were very well received and entertained. Tim Severin was shown some extremely old Icelandic books. One book was written by a Norseman in the 12th century, the "Landnambok". This tells that, when the Norsemen first reached Iceland from Scandinavia, they found living there the men whom they called "Papar", and, "they were Christian men".

Tim Severin met the President of Iceland, Dr. K. Eldjarn, who was also an authority on the history of Iceland and who told him, "We are allowed to believe that the Irish hermits were here, but we still have not found any item definitely associated with them". He went on to mention places named after the Papars, the term they called the Irish hermits.

Tim Severin and the "Brendan" were delayed a long time in Iceland because of winds blowing in from the west for a prolonged time, and they knew that in the winter, so far north as this, there would be very little daylight. So, it was decided that the wise thing to do would be to bring their boat ashore for the winter and fly back home and return in the spring. No doubt St. Brendan and his monks did the same thing on some of the islands they found themselves on, and spent their winters there.

In the spring of 1977 Severin and the crew of the "Brendan" came back to Iceland. When they found the wind blowing in a favourable direction they left Iceland, on May 7th. When they reached the sea to the south of Greenland they experienced a bad storm and were in danger of being blown on to the ice floes near the Greenland coast. They fought hard to resist this. They saw icebergs and ice packs, (which are pieces of sharp ice floating in the sea), and which threatened the tearing of their ox-hides. In fact this actually happened and required the repair of this from the outside with some spare ox-hide they were carrying. It was an admirable feat. Very probably St. Brendan and his monks underwent many misfortunes as well. They also carried extra ox-hide.

The "Navigatio" described St. Brendan and his monks encountering strange "huge, white pillars, square in shape" floating in the sea--no doubt icebergs.

Tim Severin and his crew finally touched N. America. It was Peckford Island, just off the coast of Newfoundland where they arrived on June 26th 1977. Great joy on board and a warm welcome from the islanders. It had been an epic feat.

The St. Brendan Voyage story ends with St. Brendan and his monks finding the "Promised Land of the Saints". They arrived on an island and were met by another holy man who said he had been stranded and on this island for many years and he said that it would be 40 days before they (the monks) would find the land they were looking for. He said that he would accompany them in their boat so that they would be able to find this land.

This land they found was a spacious land full of laden fruit trees as if in autumn. For 40 days they explored the land without finding an end to it, but they called it an island. (Notice how again the biblical term "forty days" is used to describe a long time, a common way of describing a long time in that era). They came upon a large river. St. Brendan said, "We cannot cross this river and we do not know how big this land is". (Incidentally, this land was strikingly like what had been described by the monk Barind to St. Brendan before he started his voyage).

Soon after, they met and were greeted by a young man who seemed to know their names and could speak to them. He told them that God had caused the long delay in them finding this land because He wanted to show them his secrets in the ocean. The young man (?angel) they met urged St. Brendan to return home, taking with them some fruit and precious stones of the land. He prophesied that St. Brendan would not live much longer after he returned home. In fact, this is what happened. St. Brendan and his monks set of for home and Brendan was joyously welcomed back to his monastery in Ireland.

He foretold to them that he did not have long to live and, indeed, did die soon after.

What are we to make of this whole tale? On first reading "Navigatio", written several centuries after the voyage was actually made, certain descriptions seem fanciful rather than realistic. Was this the style of writing in those days? Or were the stories turning into a sort of folk-lore? With many descriptions we can recognise whales, ice-bergs, volcanoes erupting, the Isle of the Sheep and the island of the Birds. With a few descriptions, one wonders if the author or perhaps previous raconteurs embroidered the tale? But what is important is that this tale was taken seriously at the time it was written, and even throughout the Middle Ages by many people of different nationalities, including Columbus. St. Brendan and his faithful monks certainly "stormed Heaven" with their incessant prayers all those years and it seems that Heaven brought them safely through many perilous experiences.

Did St. Brendan and his monks reach North America? There is no proof of this. But, it is entirely possible that he and/or other Irish sea-farers of that era, who had almost for certain reached Iceland, could have reached North America.

Saint Columba

St. Columba is the second of the three Irish saints of the sixth and seventh centuries I am writing about. Often he is known by his full title of "St. Columba of Iona". Iona is in Scotland, (an island off the west coast), and it was here that Columba founded the famous monastery and this was his home until he died. So, sometimes he is described as being Scottish, and in an important way he was, but he was born in Ireland and did not come to Iona until he was into his forties.

We know a good deal about Columba, not only because of traditional stories having been handed down, but mainly because of the book written about him by the historian Adamnan. It is also interesting to note that Bede of Jarrow, (northern England)--saint and historian--who lived a century and a half after Columba, mentions St. Columba in his well-known historical book. Columba was born in what is now known as Donegal, in north-western Ireland, about the year 521. He was "well-born" in the sense that he was of royal lineage on both his father's and mother's sides. Later, he became a pupil at the famous monastic school of St. Clonard Abbey in County Meath, which drew an amazing number of students and scholars to its walls, even from outside Ireland. This abbey was one of the fruits of St. Patrick's missionary work in a land seemingly eager to be converted to Christianity.

St. Columba has been described as having "a striking figure, of great stature and powerful build, with a loud, melodious voice which could be heard from one hilltop to another"! He became a deacon and then a priest and after working in Ireland for many years, his missionary zeal took him to Iona. He and 12 companions embarked in a curragh, (the same sort of vessel used by St. Brendan), from Ireland in the direction of Scotland and landed on the small island of Iona. The king of this part of Scotland, Conall, was a kinsman of Columba's and Conall gave this island to Columba for his work. Columba made this his home for the rest of his life. Here Columba founded a monastery which over the years prospered and attracted many monks to be trained and educated. Monks from Iona set up other religious centres and monasteries in different places in Europe and even as far as Switzerland. And, Iona also became a place to which people made journeys or pilgrimages. (See Endnote).

In Iona St. Columba himself became involved in the work of his life, "the conversion of the Northern Picts". Iona, situated where it was, meant that north of that latitude the people of Scotland tended to be called "Picts" and south of that line called "Scots". Columba founded monasteries and churches in different parts of northern Scotland which became centres for the Christianising of the land. He had an immense influence on people he met. People were drawn to his obvious sanctity and there were miracles associated with him. He lived an austere, ascetic life. His biographer, Adamnan, who knew him, and in fact was related to him, wrote that he slept on a bare slab of rock, ate mainly barley and oat cakes and drank only water! When he was at Iona he was usually to be found in his cell where people of all sorts visited him, in need of spiritual or material help. Adamnan further wrote:

"He had the face of an angel. He was of excellent nature, polished in speech, holy in deed, great in council. He never let a single hour pass without engaging in prayer or reading or writing or some other occupation. He endured the hardships of fasting without intermission by day and night; the burden of a single one of his labours would have seemed beyond the powers of man. And, in the middle of all his toils, he appeared loving to all, serene and holy, rejoicing in the joy of the Holy Spirit in his inmost heart".

There is the following story told about him. When Columba and his comrades approached what is now called Inverness, the formidable king of those parts, named Brude, declared that Columba and his monks were forbidden to enter. It is said that a miracle occurred, for when Columba reached the locked gates of Brude's strong-hold, he raised his arm and made the sign of the cross and the bolts fell out and the gates swung open. Brude was so impressed that he allowed them to enter. Brude and his people listened to Columba. He was moved and from then on held Columba in high esteem.

Endnote

Iona was for centuries a famous centre of Christian learning. Many early Scottish kings and chiefs and also important people from Ireland and Norway are buried in the Iona graveyard. Of interest, King Duncan of Scotland, remembered by Shakespeare, (who lost his life at the hands of Macbeth), is one who was buried there.

Saint Aidan

St. Aidan, born in the west of Ireland is often called "St. Aidan of Lindisfarne". Lindifarne is a small island, just off the coast of North East England in what was then called Northumbria. Lindisfarne monastery, founded by Aidan, became the most important Christian centre in northern England of that era.

We know a great deal about St. Aidan because he has been much written about, especially by St. Bede. As will be described later, one is really touched by Aidan's beautiful, saintly character.

We know that Aidan went from Ireland to Iona in Scotland about 630 AD, where he spent five years at the famous monastery there. A priest originally from Iona had just returned from Northumbria where he had been sent to try and revive Christianity, but he had been unsuccessful in swaying the people, complaining that, "The Angles are too stubborn." Aidan was sent to Northumbria instead. Aidan made friends with Oswald, who was by then King of Northumbria, and this friendship lasted till Oswald died. With the consent of King Oswald, Aidan founded a monastery on the island of Lindisfarne which was close to Oswald's castle at Bamburgh. In time, many monks from this monastery, travelled around northern England spreading the Christian word.

It is worth spending a little time on the subject of King Oswald. He was the son of a previous King of Northumbria who was killed in battle. While someone else was king, Oswald travelled to Ireland and Scotland, and to Iona, He studied, (and learned to speak Irish), and became a converted Christian. He finally became King and gave great help to St. Aidan's reforming work. He was killed in battle. He is venerated in England as a martyr and a saint. It is no wonder that he and Aidan became so close.

Oswald's successor was King Oswin, who also became very friendly with Aidan. (Interestingly enough, after he died, Oswin was also venerated in England as a saint and a martyr.)

There is a story told that King Oswin gave Aidan a horse to help him in his work and travel. Aidan was accustomed to walk from one village to another, conversing politely with whoever he met and slowly getting them interested in Christianity. Not long after he was given the horse, Aidan, noted for his charitable acts, felt such sympathy for a certain needy beggar that he gave him the horse! When King Oswin heard about this, he was incensed, but it was not long before their friendship was restored!

Yes. We do indeed have many writings of old describing St. Aidan's admirable character and the miracles attributed to him. It has been said that Aidan lived a frugal life and encouraged the laity to fast and to study the scriptures. He himself fasted on Wednesdays and Fridays and seldom ate at the "royal" table. The gifts he was given he tended to soon give away to the needy, or he used them to buy the freedom of slaves, some of whom entered religious life. During Lent Aidan would retire to the small island of Farne for penance and prayer. St. Bede wrote in his biography of Aidan, that "he was a pontiff inspired with a passionate love of virtue, but at the same time, full of a surpassing mildness and gentleness".

Saint Leo (Pope Leo the Great)

Pope Leo 1 lived in the 5th century. He died in 461. He has been known as "Pope Leo the Great" since soon after he died. It is interesting to know that there have been just two popes who were called "the Great", the other one being Pope Gregory 1, who died in 604. (See Endnote.) Gregory was also canonised a saint. Leo was not just a man of prayer and courage, but also he used his strong mental faculties to the fullest for the tasks that came his way. It is also written that Leo had particular trust in St. Peter for Heavenly aid.

One of the epithets that has often been used to describe Leo is, "He was absolutely unafraid of anyone or anything". Nothing stood in his way when he felt something important had to be done. One of the many stories about him tells how he confronted Attila, the fierce leader of the Huns. The Huns, from a land which is now Germany, had a strong army and they were aggressive to the point of wanting to sack and destroy Rome. They had already burnt many towns and cities on the way.

In the year 452 they marched towards Rome and what did Pope Leo do? He rode out on a horse to the army and spoke to Attila. After their talk Attila agreed to make peace and left. It is said that, later, Attila stated that while he was talking to Leo, he could see what seemed like two figures standing each side of Leo. Some have surmised from certain evidence that these figures were probably St. Peter and St. Paul. Is this a proven fact? All I can say is that miracles or "unexplainable" events have happened since our world began and will continue to do so, and there is no reason to say that this story is untrue.

However, three years later, other vandals from the north came and partially destroyed Rome. But Leo intervened, prevented the city from being burnt and saved the people from being slaughtered. He worked alongside others to rebuild the destroyed churches and buildings.

Leo was famous during his lifetime for his great writings and sermons and they are still admired. It is amazing to think that even though he lived as long ago as the 400s A.D., a large number of his letters and sermons are still preserved in Rome.

St. Leo, because of his great charity, humility and tireless efforts for peace and understanding, was a greatly loved man at the time he died.

Endnote

There is another pope who may in time be officially called "the Great". For already, Pope John Paul 11 is being spoken of in this way by many.

Saint Benedict

Benedict is not an uncommon name in religious circles. It all started from the great St. Benedict of Nursia, who was an unusually wise man. He was born about 480 A.D. Yes. As most people know our present pope is named after the saint and he is the 16th pope to be so named. Many monasteries and abbeys still in existence have been named after him, a few of them actually founded by this man. A huge number of Benedectine monasteries existed in the Middle Ages.

Benedict was born into the aristocracy of Rome. Often one reads of famous saints having been born into noble, well-off families. This seems to tell us something important right away about these individuals. It takes someone special to forsake what could be an easy life to enter a life, which right from the beginning only promises such things as poverty, obedience, chastity, hardship and prayer.

As a young man Benedict was sickened by seeing the ungodly behaviour of the Roman society of the time. This, coupled with his growing love of the Christian Gospels made him escape from Rome at an age of only about 19 or 20. He became a type of hermit in the hills not far from Rome. He was joined by others of the same mind; a community was formed, living a life of prayer during which time Benedict matured spiritually and mentally. They lived off the land. His goodness and wisdom became known around and some members of a nearby monastery who had lost their abbot, spoke to him and asked him to become their abbot. Benedict hesitated to join this monastery, for it had a bad name. But, after a while, he did agree to join it and become its abbot. The monastery was lax and they did not take easily to his attempts at reform, and, in fact, his life was threatened, and he had to leave.

A story has been told down the centuries, (which, of course, must have originated from Benedict himself). This story has been written about by many, including the great St. Gregory, to whom we are indebted to for so much of the history of the period. The story shows "the stuff that Benedict was made of". It must have been in the early days of St. Benedict, possibly when he was on his own, living as a hermit. Benedict was assailed by strong sexual temptations and memories of a woman he once knew which he could not drive out of his mind, so he flung off his clothes and threw himself into a clump of stinging nettles growing nearby. This act, this decision that he suddenly made, strengthened him. He later told his disciples "that the temptation of lust was so conquered in him that he never again felt the same thing".

The story just told of Benedict when a young man tells us about the strong spirituality that he was developing, and one is not surprised that numerous miracles were ascribed to Benedict throughout his life.

Benedict founded a monastery of his own and became abbot, and then others. Men flocked to him to become monks, because of his fame for wisdom and sanctity. His concept of an ideal monastery was so wise and proved so successful that most religious communities throughout those Middle Age centuries adopted his concept and ideas. He studied the "Rules" of other monastic orders before he formed his own. The wisdom of his "Rule" is of two kinds, the spiritual, (how to live a life on earth, following Jesus Christ), and secondly, in practical terms, how a monastery should be run. One could mention here that in one of the spiritual exhortations of St. Benedict to his monks during the season of Lent, he told them that "life should always have a Lenten character about it, because the Christian is always journeying from the old realm of sin and death to the light and love of God's kingdom".

So, Benedict founded a religious order, the Benedictines, just as well-known today as, for instance, the Franciscans or Jesuits. These religious orders have a lot in common, for instance the insistence on poverty, obedience and chastity. Also, the monk or member of such a society does not have, or hardly has, any personal possessions. What he uses or enjoys is communal.

The Benedictine rule is well-balanced. It does not call for a highly austere life-style. In the Benedictine monastery the day's activities are divided into prayer and work, not an excess of either. The work can consist of farming or gardening or some kind of outdoor activity. (The monastery has to be self-sufficient). Or, the work can consist of household chores. Or if an individual has a particular bent, it might consist of making wine, high art, writing or doing academic research. Examples of this that come to mind are, first, the famous liqueur, the "Benedictine" liqueur", and secondly I think of one of my favourite cheeses , the Oka cheese, made not far from here at the Oka monastery in Quebec, just over the border from Ontario. Work is considered a kind of prayer. Many of us know of the famous Benedectine dictum, "Laborare est orare"—"To work is to pray." It has been said that the Benedictines were the first people in history to claim that work is sacred.

It is easy to overlook and forget the good the Benedictine and other monasteries conferred on the societies of the Middle Ages. Monasteries sprung up in huge numbers in every country in Europe, many monasteries with famous names; and there was no shortage of monks. The local monastery tended to be a centre for hospitality, food for the poor, a bed for the traveller, a place to say a prayer in quiet. And, of great importance, monasteries tended to become centres of learning and education. There is not enough space here to describe or even name the famous monasteries that sprung up all over Europe.

In this regard, one thinks of some of the achievements of monasteries, for instance, the St. Bernard dogs developed and used by the monks of St. Bernard monastery in the Alps of Switzerland, to help find lost travellers. And one thinks of the Venerable Bede, (now St. Bede), a monk in a monastery in Jarrow in the north of England who died in 731. He has been called the greatest scholar of Saxon England and also called the father of English history. One thinks of a monk who lived in a monastery in Austria in the 1800s, by the name of Mendel, who has become famous for his research into heredity after his experiments with garden peas. Mendel introduced the concept of dominant and recessive genes. One thinks of the Book of Kells, in Ireland, an extraordinarily artistic, illustrated (illuminated) book of the Gospels of the New Testament, crafted by monks. In time, the monasteries mostly disappeared, partly because of the way society evolved and sometimes because of greedy and rapacious acts of rulers and conquerors.

It is worth quoting the words of Bishop Sheen, who wrote:

> "The Benedictine order helped to preserve the traditions of Christianity throughout the Middle Ages. The Benedictines are noted for their piety and encouragement of learning. During the Middle Ages, they neglected no branch of art or learning then known. They produced many of the books written before the invention of printing in Europe".

Saint Gregory
(Pope Gregory the Great)

As already stated, there were two popes named "the Great" after their death. Pope St. Gregory was one and the other was Pope St. Leo.

St. Gregory was born in Rome in 540. He came from a wealthy Roman family. The family was noted for its piety as well as its administrative talents. Gregory experienced, as he was growing up, a strong religious atmosphere in his home. Also, he was naturally pious and it has been written that "he loved to meditate on the Scriptures and to listen attentively to the conversation of his elders, so that he was devoted to God from his youth up".

Gregory was energetic and full of enthusiasm for anything he took up, and he had a mind which was never still. He became a lawyer and showed so much promise that at the young age of 30 was made the Prefect of Rome, (the Chief Magistrate of Rome), an office he held with distinction.

When Gregory's father died he inherited land and estates. After a period of prayer he decided to leave his successful civic work and resigned his position. He became a monk. He sold the land and estates he inherited and built monasteries and helped the poor. Actually, all through his life Gregory was highly generous. He was even criticized later, when he became pope, for being overgenerous to the poor and depleting the treasury at certain times!

As a simple monk he was seen in Rome wearing worthless clothes instead of the rich robes of the Prefect of Rome. In fact, all through his life Gregory shunned riches and pomp and ceremony and he resisted every advance he was asked to make, right up to the time when he had the office of pope thrust on him. As a monk he followed the usual duties and also accomplished notable writings, which included lectures on the book of Job.

Gregory's talents and energy were so evident that the pope (Pope Pelagius) called for him to leave the monastery and become a sort of papal nuncio or ambassador at the imperial court of Constantinople. Gregory did not like this type of work. After several years he returned to Rome and became abbot of a monastery in Rome during which time the pope used him as an important advisor.

At that time Gregory became acquainted with a number of English youth who were in Rome at the time. They were probably slaves of the Roman Empire, for England was at the time still under the rule of the Caesars of Rome. Gregory was struck by the good appearance of these English youth, with their fair complexion and fair hair, and he enquired who they were. He was told that they were "Angles". The story goes that Gregory's comment was, "They are indeed worthy to become angels of God", one of the earliest "puns" recorded! Gregory was saddened to hear that these youth were pagans, not Christians. It is said that Gregory's heart went out to these English youth and he sheltered them in his house, which had become a monastery.

From the time that Gregory encountered these English youth, he was determined to try and convert this pagan England to Christianity. He obtained permission from the pope to lead a number of other monks to England for this purpose. They set out and had only traveled for three days when they were caught up by a group of men sent from Rome. They stopped Gregory and brought them back to Rome. Gregory was considered too valuable a person to be lost to Rome while he was evangelizing England.

Then later, when Gregory was pope, he sent St. Augustine and 40 fellow monks to England (in 595). (This Augustine has come down in history as St. Augustine of Canterbury, not to be confused with the famous St. Augustine of Hippo.) So, not only has St. Augustine been given the credit of being the evangelist of the English but also Pope St. Gregory.

Gregory was pope for 14 years. Much has been written about his accomplishments. He has been greatly loved. In a short account it is not possible to do justice to all Pope St. Gregory did. He aided in the conversion not just of England, but also parts of Italy, Spain and the French Goths. There are 14 books of his writings. He was famous for the sermons he preached. Some of his sermons are still extant. He made changes to the liturgies used in the mass and in church services. The music accompanying the mass was changed and parts of the "Gregorian chant" are still sometimes sung in churches. And one cannot just dwell on the greatness of his mind, but one should remember his compassion and help for the poor and hungry and his protection of Jewish rights. He deserved the title "the Great".

The Venerable Bede (Saint Bede)

The Venerable Bede was born in 672 or 673 and died in 735. Since he died he has become a famous historical figure, mostly because he was studious and scholarly and wrote over 60 books, including one famous one. But in addition, he was saintly in that he truly loved Jesus Christ and the Holy Scriptures and offered his life work up to God.

Because of the former attribute, he was made a "Doctor" of the Church. And because of the latter attribute, he was called "Venerable" within two generations of his death; and he was made a saint, canonised in 1899.

Because he was known as "Venerable Bede" for so long a time, even after being canonised a saint, it is still difficult to think of him by any other title than Venerable.

Regarding his scholarly contributions to the world, one biographer wrote that "he wrote scientific, historical and theological works". Another biographer wrote that, "In point of scholarship, he was undoubtedly the most learned man of his time". The book that he is most famous for is a history of Christianity in England from its very beginning up to his day, (600 years.) Its proper name, (for he wrote in Latin), is the "Historia Ecclesiastica Gentis Anglorum", which translated is, "Ecclesiastical History of the English Nation". Although he wrote this primarily from the point of view of the development of Christianity in England during this period, the book also describes the general history of those centuries and is relied on by historians as the main source of knowledge as to what happened during that period. The great King Alfred of England, who reigned in the century after Bede, ordered that this book be translated into Anglo-Saxon. Although the native language of Bede was Anglo-Saxon, yet he became fluent in Latin at an early age and most of his writings were in Latin.

Bede was born not far from the monastery where he lived his life, the Jarrow monastery, (official title-- the monastery of Wearmouth and Jarrow), situated in northern England, close to what is now Newcastle on Tyne. (See Endnote 2.) We learn from the pen of Bede himself the following, "I was given by the care of my relations to the most reverend Abbot Benedict to be educated. From that time, I have spent the whole of my life within that monastery, devoting all my pains to the study of the Scriptures, and amid the observance of monastic discipline and the daily charge of singing in the church, it has been ever my delight to learn or teach or write". Bede was ordained a deacon at the age of nineteen and a priest at the age of thirty.

When he was young, Bede suffered from the handicap of a speech impediment. At around that time, the legend of Bishop Cuthbert, who lived about one generation before Bede, (and who also lived in that north-eastern part of England), was spreading widely around the land. It had been said that miraculous healings had been ascribed to the intercession of Bishop Cuthbert. Bede earnestly prayed to Cuthbert to intercede for him in Heaven. His prayers were answered. One of the many biographies that St. Bede wrote was the life of Bishop Cuthbert.

Bede's famous book, "Ecclesiastical History of the English Nation" was not only scholarly, but many have described it as fascinating and thoroughly readable. It is clear to those who have read it that it must have been a work of love for Bede. Bede went to a great deal of trouble to get his facts right. He arranged for learned people with access to libraries all over England to help with his research.

It is clear from the writings of his fellow monks in the monastery, especially from descriptions of the last days of his life, that he was greatly loved for his simplicity, gentleness and piety. One of his disciples, Cuthbert, wrote, "I can with truth declare that I never saw with my eyes or heard with my ears anyone give thanks so unceasingly to God". Even on the day that he died, Bede was still busy dictating a translation of the Gospel of St. John into Anglo-Saxon. This dictation was written down by the boy Wilbert,who, after Bede had paused for an unusual amount of time, spoke to the saint, saying, "There is still one sentence, dear master, which is still not written down". This Bede did eventually write, and then he requested that he be moved into a chair close to "any holy place where I used to pray, that so sitting, I may call on my Father". And, not long after, while whispering a prayer, he breathed his last. That was on the Vigil of the Ascension, May 25, 735.

Endnotes.

1. Bede was the only Englishman made a "Doctor" of the Church. And, also, Bede was the only Englishman mentioned in Dante's great work, "Paradise".

2. The Jarrow monastery had between 300 and 500 books in it at that time--a source of amazement, such a long time before the advent of the printing press, and demonstrating the importance of monasteries as centres of learning. (See the story of St. Benedict.)

3. From the personal point of view, I, the writer, could add that when I was serving in the British Navy at the end of and just after the Second World War, the ship I was on longer than any other, (in the Pacific), was H.M.S. Venerable. Maybe I am mistaken, but I have always fondly wondered if the person or persons who chose the name "Venerable" for the ship had Bede at the back of their minds! "Venerable" is an unusual name for a warship.

Saint Boniface

One often remembers some saints by certain well-known, isolated features or events in their lives. For instance, one can easily connect the picture of a knight seated on a horse, taking off his coat and handing it down to a poor beggar freezing with the cold with St. Martin of Tours; or, St. George, mythically portrayed as a warrior on horseback, striking a dragon with a long lance; or, if we see a clover leaf with its three leaves, perhaps we think of St. Patrick. Often, St. Boniface has been depicted with an axe in his hand. Why an axe? I will tell you later.

St. Boniface is the patron saint of Germany and Holland. He is known as "The apostle of Germany". So it is surprising perhaps to learn that he was born in England (in Devonshire) and did not leave England until he was in his forties.

St. Boniface's real name was Wynfrith. Yes, that sounds like an Anglo-Saxon name. He was born about 675 A.D. to prominent citizens in a place called Crediton. At a fairly young age he was drawn to a religious life because of his admiration for the monks he had met. His parents at first resisted, but later agreed to him entering a monastery nearby. He prospered and was well-thought of by his superiors. From a simple monk he later became a priest and made a name for himself as a teacher and preacher. As the years went by, his longing to go and evangelise and become a Christian missionary in lands where there was no Christianity came more and more to the fore, and although his abbot did not want to see such a valuable priest leave, he finally gave in and Wynfrith set sail for the land of the Frisians, (part of Holland).

However, not long after he arrived in this part of Holland the local pagan king declared war on the Christians, destroyed the churches and monasteries they had built and drove them out. So, Wynfrith returned to England, but he did not lose his determination to return to the work of being a Christian missionary. This time he travelled to Rome to get the blessing and commission of the pope, Pope Gregory 11. He spent a whole winter in Rome. The pope got to know Wynfrith and was impressed by him. He changed his name to "Boniface" and sent him off to Thuringia in Germany.

It is easy to overlook the fact that travel was difficult in the extreme in those days. It would have been far easier for Boniface to have spent the rest of his life in Devonshire, England. To get to Germany from Rome meant a long journey on primitive roads or tracts; and it meant crossing part of the Alps, either on a horse or on foot or perhaps at times in some sort of carriage on wheels. And, also, of course, he faced the daunting task of trying to convert pagan people, who might not just be stubborn and difficult to change, but could be very aggressive against foreigners coming and trying to change their ways.

Boniface spent 35 years, until he died, doing missionary work in Germany and to a lesser extent in Holland. It was obviously slow work at first but his efforts paid off in time. Like in most countries of Europe the people seemed to be ready to warmly accept Christianity. He was a dedicated worker in this field. He and his fellow-workers converted huge numbers of people.

Two of his fellow-workers were his nephews, Winibald and Willibald, outstanding men, who joined their uncle when they were young and later were canonised. It is clear from the letters we still have, written to Boniface and from him, that he asked for help from abbesses and abbots in England and was sent nuns and monks. One of the nuns who joined him in Germany was his niece, Walburga, the sister of Winibald and Willibald. She was also an outstanding person and became a remarkable saint.

Boniface usually started his conversion work by trying to convert the leaders and rulers. One of these was the famous Pepin. (See Endnotes.) In time, the pope made Boniface Bishop of part of Germany, and in 722 he was made Bishop of the whole of Germany, based at Mainz.

Now, what about this axe? Some of the people whom the missionaries were trying to convert were attracted to Christianity but many were reluctant to give up their superstitions and adherence to heathen "gods" such as Odin, Thor, Valkyrie and others. At a place called Geisman, the Christians had already built a church and a monastery. Nearby was the oak tree of Thor, (the God of Thunder), which the pagan non-Christians worshipped and believed to be sacred. Boniface let it be known that he was going to cut down this tree. While he himself was using an axe to fell this tree, people gathered around expecting to see some reaction from their gods, but even when the tree finally fell, nothing happened. Hence, the pictures of St. Boniface holding an axe.

Boniface, like many missionaries whom the Church has canonised as 'saints', never gave up, even into old age. When he was nearly 80 he went with about 30 companions to the Frisia part of Holland where he had been 40 years before. But, on June 5, 755, near the modern town of Dokkum, they were all massacred by heathen ruffians. His body was taken back to the monastery he had founded at Fulda, in central Germany, where a magnificent cathedral now encloses his tomb.

It is right what has been said, "The blood of the martyrs was the seed which grew the church".

Boniface is revered in Germany. As one historian wrote, "Everything which has developed afterwards in Germany, in the realm of politics, the church and spirituality, is established on the foundation laid by Boniface, whose tomb should be more sacred for us than the tombs of the patriarchs and prophets were for the Jews, because he is truly the spiritual father of our people".

Endnotes.

1. Pepin was the father of Charlemagne the Great, who was to become the first "Holy Roman Emperor". He was "King of the Franks" from 768 to 814 AD.
2. Personal. I, the author, happened to be born in Devonshire, England, and, no doubt, this is partly why I enjoyed reading and writing about St. Boniface!

3. The following is an excerpt from a letter of St. Boniface, who wrote:

   "In her voyage across the ocean of this world, the Church is like a ship pounded by the waves of life's different stresses. Our duty is not to abandon ship, but to keep her on course."

Saint Walburga

St. Walburga is perhaps a saint you never heard of before reading this book and reading about her uncle, St. Boniface. I had reason to look her up recently and found that she was a most lovable and remarkable person, and certainly not to be classed as a "minor" saint; and further reading showed me that she was part of a saintly, heroic and dedicated family. As already told in this book, her uncle, (the brother of her mother), was no other than the great St. Boniface. Walburga and her two older brothers, Willibald and Winibald, also both later canonised, joined their uncle St. Boniface in what is now Germany, which was at that time pagan. These four individuals of the one family have been greatly admired and revered in Germany ever since as Christian evangelisers.

It is interesting to note what a very short time it took for the conversion of England to Christanity to become a deep and fervent conversion. For St. Boniface was born about 675, and St. Walburga about 710, and it had been only in 595 that St. Augustine of Canterbury with his monks arrived in southern England from Rome. In that short time there were countless English devotees of Christ, some of whom risked all to evangelise parts of Europe, and others who risked or lost their lives in pilgrimages or crusades to the Holy Land. And, also in that time, monasteries and abbeys, noted for piety and learning, started to spring up in England.

Walburga's father, Richard, was a chieftain or lord in Devonshire, England. He, accompanied by his two sons, went on a pilgrimage to the Holy Land when Walburga was 11 years old and she was placed in an abbey not far away, (Winborne, Dorset). She stayed on there well after the usual age and, in fact, stayed for 26 years, becoming a nun at the accustomed age. She was both spiritually and mentally strong, with leadership qualities, and was fluent in the Latin language. Incidentally, due to the fact that in later life she wrote a "vita" (a life) of her beloved brother Winibald and also an account of her brother Willibald's travels in Palestine, (both in Latin, of course), she is often credited with being the first female author in England and Germany!

Walburga's uncle, St. Boniface, and his followers were very successful in the work of converting Germany. But, he needed more help. His two nephews, Winibald and Willibald were already with him. He wrote to the Abbess of Winborne Abbey asking for nuns. Abbess Tetta sent many nuns, one being Walburga.

Walburga was an exceptional person. So many stories have been told about marvels connected with her. One story goes thus. It was when she and the nuns accompanying her were on the boat, bound for the continent of Europe, that a terrible storm suddenly started up. Walburga got down on to her knees on the deck of the boat and started praying. The prayers said by her were held responsible for the fact that the wind suddenly died down and the boat reached shore safely. The sailors on the boat were so impressed by what they called a miracle, that they could not keep quiet about it, and, after landing, Walburga was welcomed with joy and veneration. She suddenly became famous. Not long after they landed, the nuns were delayed in Antwerp, (Belgium), close by. They were delayed there long enough for the people there to get to know and love Walburga.

She was in the habit of praying in the church there, (now named after her.) This church has gone through various changes and upheavals over the centuries. At one time, a painting of the boat which survived the storm used to hang in the church. This picture was painted by Peter Rubens in 1610. And, this church used to celebrate the feast of St. Walburga four times a year. Walburga evidently possessed a charisma and people she was in contact with soon recognised her saintly qualities.

Walburga and her group of nuns journeyed on into Germany and reached Mainz and were warmly welcomed by Boniface and Walburga's brother Willibald. Winibald was, at the time elsewhere in Germany.

It was not long after Walburga had been working in an abbey in Germany that she was transferred to become the Abbess of the abbey at Heidenheim. Her favourite brother Winibald governed a monastery nearby. After his death, she was in charge of the monastery as well as her own abbey. It seems that wherever she went she was very highly regarded. Readers will probably remember that Walburga wrote a biography (a "vita") of her beloved brother Winibald.

It has been written that Walburga possessed "virtue, sweetness and prudence, which were added to the gifts of grace and nature". Many miracles were attributed to her. When she died, (at Heidenheim), her body was laid to rest beside that of her brother, Winibald. A little later, due to an accidental desecration at the burial site, her remains and that of her brother were transferred to Eichstadt, "and many wonders occurred at the tombs". (See Endnotes).

Endnotes

1. (Personal). When I arrived with my wife in Canada I went, as a doctor, to work in a small town in northern Saskatchewan by the name of St. Walburg! The original settlers of this area came from many different countries, but probably the majority were from Germany, so I assumed for many years that St. Walburga must have been born in Germany. More recently I discovered that she was born in England, but, in a sense, one can well call her German in that she spent the bulk of her life in Germany and died there.

2. Many biographers of St Walburga over the centuries have described the strange occurrence of an "oil" or "dew" or a "liquid' flowing from the grave of St. Walburga. Other instances of this phenomenon have been recorded, connected with other saints. There are many claims that prayers to St. Walburga, using the "oil" and asking her to intercede in Heaven, have been answered.

Saint Wenceslas

St. Wenceslas, (sometimes spelt Wenceslaus), was a King (or Duke), a saint and a sort of martyr. He is the main patron saint of the Czech Republic.

He was a champion of Christianity in the early years of what was then called Bohemia. He was murdered for religious and political reasons, mainly because he strove hard to make and keep Bohemia a Christian land, hence the appellation of "martyr".

He won fame as a "good" man. He is still famous for his goodness to this day. This can be seen in different ways. For instance, there is the well-known Christmas carol. "Good King Wenceslas". Also, there has come down through the centuries words of praise that he was "full of virtue". There is the following description of him. "He was, by God's grace, a man of utmost faith. He was charitable to the poor and he would clothe the naked, feed the hungry and offer hospitality to travelers according to the summons of the Gospel. He would not allow widows to be treated unjustly. He loved all his people, both rich and poor".

We do not know much about his life. He was probably born in 903. We do know that he was mainly brought up by his grandmother. She was a saintly person and actually was later canonized, (St. Ludmilla). His father, who was Duke of Bohemia, died when Wenceslas was only 13 and Wenceslas took over the leadership of the land when he became 18. He made a vow of celibacy and did not marry. He died at a young age. He was murdered at the instigation of a younger brother, probably about the age of 32, when he was on his way to church.

So, we see the story of a person who was not just a pious Christian but a person who was courageous enough to risk his life to try and lift his land out of paganism into Christianity.

Coming back to the well-known Christmas carol I have already mentioned, it is worthwhile quoting a bit of it and describing the story it tells. The first verse goes:

> "Good King Wenceslas looked out, on the Feast
>   of Stephen, (*Day after Christmas*)
> When the snow lay round about, deep and crisp
>   and even:
> Brightly shone the moon that night, tho' the frost
>   was cruel,
> When a poor man came in sight, gath'ring winter
>   fuel."

The story goes on to tell how King Wenceslas is wondering who is this "poor man". He asks the page who is with him, "Yonder peasant who is he?" He is told, "Sire, he lives a good league hence". The King decides to invite the poor man to dinner and he instructs the page,

"Bring me flesh, and bring me wine, bring me
    pine logs hither;
Thou and I will see him dine when we bear them
    thither".

The King and the page have to trudge back with
pine logs "through the wild wind's lament and the bitter
weather". The page is afraid of the terrible night and feels
he can go on no longer:

"Sire, the night is darker now and the wind blows
    stronger;
Fails my heart, I know not how; I can go no
    longer".

But he is encouraged by the King to press on and
follow in his footsteps:

"Mark my footsteps, my good page. Tread thou
    in them boldly.
Thou shalt find the winter's rage freeze thy blood
    less coldly".

The words of the carol end with:

"Therefore, Christian men, be sure, wealth or
    rank possessing,
Ye who now will bless the poor, shall yourselves
    find blessing".

Saint Stephen, King of Hungary

St. Stephen was born about 975. His father was the third Duke to govern the Magyars. Stephen's mother, already a Christian and a true one, took great care of her son's training. At the age of 11, Stephen and his father were baptised Christians when Archbishop Adalbert of Prague, (later St. Adalbert), was on a preaching mission in Hungary. It was then that Stephen received the name of "Stephen", named after the first Christian martyr, St. Stephen, (stoned to death just outside Jerusalem.) Previously he had been called Vaik.

Stephen's father recognised his son's leadership qualities and strong Christian faith and saw to it that Stephen would succeed him as Duke. When he died, Stephen was about 20 years old and for the next 40 years, Stephen was monarch of the Hungarians. He was at first a Duke and then, in 1001, Pope Sylvester, impressed by the achievements and character of Stephen, bestowed on him the title of King of Hungary, after sending him a crown from Rome, the famous crown of St. Stephen.

The pope sent this crown to Stephen in the care of Astricius. Stephen met Astricius in Gran (in Hungary) and, with great reverence, listened to the official message from the pope. The pope confirmed and approved the churches and monasteries built by Stephen and the ordination of the bishops. Astricius, with solemnity, anointed and crowned Stephen Christian King of Hungary. This crown, later known as the Holy Crown of Hungary, has had an interesting history. (See Endnote).

During Stephen's reign he made important church and secular changes and reforms, for Hungary was in a disorganised state in both these respects. He did all he could to make Hungary a Christian country, for Hungary was to quite an extent pagan and somewhat savage at the time. He brought into Hungary priests and Benedictine monks from other countries to help evangelise and educate. Some of these men lost their lives as martyrs, going about their work. He built churches and monasteries and convents, the most famous of these monasteries being the one named after St. Martin, which had been started by his father and which he completed. He founded dioceses and appointed bishops as the land became more converted.

On the secular side, Stephen formed counties with governors to rule them. He established good laws and magistrates.

In an admirable and unusual way, King Stephen sometimes mingled, (in disguise), among the ordinary people. He did this without any bodyguard. Sometimes he was disguised as a missionary and gave out alms to the poor. Mostly he just wanted to find out what were the greatest needs of the people. On one occasion, when he was dispensing alms, he was set upon. He was physically attacked in a brutal way, knocked down and his purse of money was snatched from him. Afterwards, he took this painful attack in good humour! When the nobles heard this story, they persuaded to him to give up this dangerous practice!

There is no doubt but that Stephen was a deeply committed Christian. He was a man of prayer, fasting and alms giving. We are told that through his life, he "had Christ on his lips, Christ in his heart and Christ in all he did." When he became ruler, he placed his country under the protection of the Virgin Mary and regularly kept the feast of Mary's Assumption with great affection. He admired St. Martin of Tours greatly and chose him as his patron saint.

Stephen's wars were essentially wars of defence when he came under attack by those who opposed his regime. One of the strongest attacks came from a powerful army of pagans who were angry at the inroads being made by this Christian religion. In this particular battle Stephen took part himself and prepared for it by fasting and prayer and a much bigger army was defeated by him. He was successful in repulsing all the attacks on him and successful in his attempt to unite the Magyars.

Towards the end of his life, Stephen lost his beloved son, Emeric, who died of a mortal wound suffered while he was hunting. Stephen mourned him deeply and he lost some of his vitality from then on. He had been getting his son ready to succeed him as king. Emeric was well-fitted to be a good king.

Before Emeric died, Stephen wrote a letter to him, at the time he was preparing Emeric to take over from him.

It is worth quoting part of this letter for it is a touching letter and also it clearly shows the nobility of Stephen's character:

> My dearest son, if you desire to honour the royal crown, I advise, I urge you, above all things, to maintain the Catholic and Apostolic faith with such diligence and care that you may be an example for all those placed under you by God; and that all the clergy may rightly call you a man of true Christian profession.

> My beloved son, delight of my heart, hope of your posterity, I pray, I command, that at every time, strengthened by your devotion to me, you may show favour not only to relations and kin, or to the most eminent, be they leaders or rich men or fellow-countrymen, but also to foreigners and to all who welcome you. Be patient with everyone, not only with the powerful, but also with the weak.

> Finally, be strong lest prosperity lift you up too much or adversity cast you down. Be humble in this life that God may raise you up in the next. Be truly moderate and do not punish or condemn anyone immoderately. Be gentle so that you may never oppose justice. Be honourable so that you never voluntarily bring disgrace upon anyone. Be chaste, so that you may avoid all the foulness that so resembles the pangs of death.

> All these virtues I have noted above make up the royal crown and without them no one is fit

to rule here on earth or attain to the heavenly Kingdom.

St. Stephen died on the feast of the Assumption 1038, his favourite feast day. After his death, healing miracles were said to have occurred at his tomb. He was canonised shortly after his death, in 1083. He is venerated as the patron saint of Hungary.

Endnote.

The Crown of St. Stephen was recovered from the Nazis in 1945 at the end of the World War 11. They had seized it during their occupation of Hungary. It was placed in the custody of the United States Government until 1978, when it was returned to Hungary by order of President Jimmy Carter. It has been enshrined in the Hungarian parliament building in Budapest.

Saint Anselm

St. Anselm–one cannot help admiring and loving him as a warm human being as soon as one starts reading about him. He was also renowned as a Christian scholar. He had a strong love for Christ and his Church, and he liked to delve into the inner truths of Christianity and Philosophy. He has been called the most learned theologian of his generation. And, another attribute--he fought hard in the latter part of his life to uphold the rights of the Church against its opponents.

In a sense, one feels sympathy for the role Anselm had to play in this latter part of his life, which he certainly did not choose, for he, essentially a humble, scholarly monk, found himself thrust into the role of defender of the Church against the ruthless attempts of two English kings, King William 11 and King Henry 1, (especially the former), who were bent on using the Church to further their own interests. For, Anselm became Archbishop of Canterbury, England in 1093 and died sixteen years later in 1109.

Anselm was born of highly ranked parents in Burgundy, (northern Italy), about 1033. He had a pious mother, and no doubt, influenced by her, expressed the wish to be admitted to a monastery at the age of 15, but his father refused this. His father was stern and harsh to the extent that, after his mother died and life became intolerable, Anselm left home. He traveled a long way, to Normandy in northern France, to the well-known Benedictine monastery of Bec, where he was accepted as a monk at the age of 27. There, he met and came under the influence of the great Lanfranc, who also originated from northern Italy and who, at the time was Prior of Bec. (Lanfranc, with his great leadership qualities later became Archbishop of Canterbury and due to his saintliness was later canonised by the Church.)

Three years after Anselm arrived at Bec, Lanfranc was appointed Abbot of a nearby abbey and Anselm took Lanfranc's position as Prior, a very short time after arriving. Anselm had impressed everyone with his talents and character but this rapid promotion did cause some jealousy among his confreres. But, as a result of Anselm's wisdom, sensitivity and humility, he, before long, received the allegiance and support of his fellow monks. He was Prior for 15 years and then became Abbot of Bec.

It was while he was at Bec that William the Conqueror was dying. William was the King of England, but was in Normandy at the time. It is a measure of how highly Anselm was regarded as a wise and holy monk that, on his death bed, William asked if Anselm could come and be with him and "give him consolation".

The next step for Anselm was to England. One could almost say that he was forcibly made Archbishop of

Canterbury! The previous Archbishop was his old friend Lanfranc but Lanfranc had died three years previously. For those three years the see of Canterbury had been vacant. There had been no Archbishop. It was deliberately kept vacant by King William 11, (often called William Rufus), who had seized the possessions of the see and pocketed the Church revenues for himself. King William 11 was the third son of William the Conqueror, who was king before him. He was a harsh ruler and according to the Anglo-Saxon Chronicle was "hated by all his people". During those three years, after Lanfranc died, the nobles, the bishops and the clergy of England found it imperative for there to be a Church leader for many reasons, and especially to stand up against the ruthless actions of the king. But, the king "swore that neither Anselm nor anyone else should be Archbishop as long as he lived".

Anselm had been making visits to England on several occasions, but he was reluctant to do so, for he did not want it to be thought that he was interested in the position of Archbishop; and in point of fact he did not feel he was fit or worthy for what would certainly take him into a political, secular situation–and a stormy one. At his age he wanted to remain the Abbot of Bec. He had spent his life as a monk, as an abbot and as a writer of philosophy and theology.

It happened that Anselm was urgently requested for help and advice and to go to the Earl of Chester in England when matters came to a head regarding the vacant see of Canterbury. The bishops and people of England overwhelmingly wanted no one else but Anselm to be Archbishop, but when approached, Anselm resisted strongly. It is somewhat confusing to glean the exact historical facts, but when Anselm finally said that he would consider this matter provided that the king would give back the possessions he had stolen from the Church and agree to some other points, he was physically taken to a meeting, with the king present, and after various points had been thrashed out, he was consecrated Archbishop on December 4, 1093.

It was not long before William broke his promises. His brother Robert was the ruler of the duchy of Normandy and he and William were on bad terms. King William was planning to send an army to take over the Duchy and he needed money. Anselm had to resist the King's attempts to plunder the Church for these monies. Anselm also had to fight tenaciously for the Church in order to make reforms which were needed and which the King opposed, and to maintain control of the abbeys and monasteries which were under the Church's jurisdiction. King William did everything he could to get rid of Anselm. It happened that Anselm went to Rome in 1097 to confer with the pope, Pope Urban 11; and when he wanted to return, King William refused to have him back. The Church in England was in a state of anarchy and William was profiting by it. Anselm was still in Europe when the king was killed on August 2, 1100.

King William 11 (William Rufus) was succeeded by King Henry 1, (who was the youngest son of William the Conqueror). Henry wanted Anselm back in Canterbury and wrote to him saying that he "committed to be counselled by Anselm". But, during Henry's reign Anselm was again involved in disputes with the king. Henry also tried to use the Church for his own interests whenever it suited him. But there was more peace than with King

William 11. There were several instances when they were able to actually assist each other.

The last two years for Anselm at Canterbury were comparatively peaceful. He continued to follow his duties as Archbishop with prudence and care for his flock until he died in 1107. St. Anselm deserves praise for the way he stood up courageously and successfully against the strong attempts of King William and King Henry to exploit the Church. St. Anselm also deserves much praise, for while he was Archbishop of Canterbury in the last 16 years of his life, by his example, wisdom and spirituality, he "helped heal the wounds of the conquest of the English by the Normans."

St. Anselm's accomplishments in the field of philosophy and theology earned him a Doctorate of the Church, (in 1720). Much of his writings were done when he was in Bec monastery. And, while he was in Bec and due to his leadership, teaching and example, Bec "became the foremost seat of learning in Europe, attracting students from Italy and elsewhere".

Regarding the huge number of Anselm's writings one can mention the following. He wrote a whole book on "Why God became Man", (in Latin–"Cur Deus Homo"). In this he explained the wisdom, justice and necessity of "Why God became Man", (the Incarnation of Christ). And he wrote a treatise on "Original Sin". Then, in another of his writings he painstakingly elaborated on this fact–that to be able to truly understand Christian doctrine, one has to have *belief* in Christ and Christianity. Put another way and in his own exact words, (written in Latin, of course), "Unless I first believe I shall not understand". There had already been much written by other authors on the subject of the existence of God. In one book Anselm reviewed all that had been written on this, and in another he put forward his own "proof" for this belief.

St. Anselm died on Wednesday of Holy Week, (April 21, 1109) among his monks at Canterbury. Some may be interested in the fact that Anselm's name is one of the illustrious few mentioned in Dante's "Divine Comedy".

Endnotes.

One is full of admiration for St. Anselm and all the many other writers of those early centuries before paper and the printing press came into use. Many of them wrote voluminously. They used parchment and wax tablets, difficult to write on. There is a story about the trouble Anselm had after putting an important piece of writing onto wax tablets. The tablets got broken. Anselm painstakingly put the pieces together so that the writing was readable, and then, for more security, copied them onto parchment. Writing was certainly different from nowadays!

Saint Margaret of Scotland

St. Margaret was a queen. One can remember several other kings or queens who were canonised saints. There was Queen Elizabeth (Isabella) of Portugal, King Stephen of Hungary, Queen Elizabeth of Hungary, King Edward the Confessor of England, King Louis of France and Holy Roman Emperor Henry 11.

St. Margaret became a queen but she was already of royal blood. On her father's side, her great uncle was King Edward the Confessor of England, (Saint Edward), and her mother was a Hungarian princess. Margaret married King Malcolm of Scotland, (Malcolm 111), to become Queen of Scotland. (See Endnotes).

She was a particularly fine queen who, by her personal example and by what she did, was a blessing to Scotland.

How did she meet Malcolm of Scotland? It was by accident and because of what a bad storm did to the ship she was on.

Although Margaret was born in Hungary, her family, that is her parents, she and her brother and sister, moved to England when Margaret was still a child. Margaret was the oldest of the three children. Her great-uncle, the saintly King Edward the Confessor, was King of England at the time. Then, in 1066, William of Normandy invaded England. The king of England, (Harold), was killed in the battle and William became the ruler of England. By this time Margaret's father had died. Margaret's mother, Agatha, was afraid how William might treat her and her family and decided to leave for safety to Europe.

The ship she and her family were on sailed into a bad storm which blew the ship, out of control, in a northerly direction. It is not certain where the ship finally landed up, whether it was on the coast of north east England or the coast of Scotland, but it seems that at that time King Malcolm of Scotland ruled that area. This was because for several years a considerable amount of warfare had been going on between the Scots and the English each side of the border, with raids into each others' territories.

So, Margaret's family had to throw themselves onto the mercy of King Malcolm in their hour of need. No doubt they were all lucky to be alive.

King Malcolm welcomed Agatha and family to his court. Margaret was then a young woman. It was not long before Malcolm fell in love with the beautiful princess; not only beautiful to look at but biographers have described her as also possessing a beautiful nature.

Before she left Hungary Margaret had been brought up and had been taught to be a devout Christian by Benedictine nuns. She was pious, but she was also a strong-willed and determined person. She was well-educated. She could read Latin at a young age. When Malcolm proposed marriage, she at first resisted. She was serious minded and prayerful. She had been considering entering a religious life, but then, conscious of the potential for good inherent in the position of queen and in the role of mother, she accepted. They were married, probably in 1070, in Dunfermline, (just north and west of Edinburgh). She was 22.

The Scottish nobles were rough. They tended to engage in raids into northern England and to quarrel among themselves. King Malcolm was also somewhat rough, at any rate by the standards of the English or European courts. For instance, he could not read. But he was essentially a good man. He responded to the example and influence of his wife. He continued to lead raids into northern England during his reign, many of them in retaliation for the raids by the English into Scotland, but he was a good king. Margaret taught him the ways of prayer and charity. They prayed together and on many occasions they both fed crowds of poor people with their own hands. She had a love for the poor. It has been said that she and King Malcolm both personally bathed the feet of poor visitors. He gave her free rein in many of the reforms she wished to make in the country. They had a happy marriage.

Yes. Margaret had an unusually sincere love for the poor; and, of course, many of those poor must have been ultra-poor. Among her many other acts of charity, every day in Lent, Margaret gave out with her own hands 300 meals to poor people. And she did not then go and feast on a royal dinner. Just the opposite. She consistently practiced self denial, some even said to a fault.

Margaret was a strong person, and she certainly was not idle. She accomplished a great deal in her short life.

She founded several churches, including the Abbey of Dunfermline. In it she enshrined her greatest treasure, a small relic of the cross that Jesus Christ died on. She brought English Benedictine monks to the abbey. She built schools, monasteries and pilgrimage hostels. From outside Scotland she invited textile merchants and stone masons. She arranged for a ferry to make it easier for pilgrims to cross the Firth of Forth on their way to the shrine at St. Andrews. (See Endnotes).

She called a meeting (synod) of the country's religious leaders not long after she became queen, for the Church in Scotland had fallen into lax ways. Meetings continued regularly. The proper ritual of the mass was brought back. The rules for fasting in Lent were restored. Easter Holy Communion was encouraged. Her piety allied to her determination inspired a return to the religious practices that were common in England and on the continent of Europe. Her private life was filled with prayer.

There is a statue of St. Margaret in Scotland. On it you can see her holding coins of money in her right hand and a book in her left. The coins represent the alms she was accustomed to hand out to the poor. The book carries a story. This book was a favourite of hers for it was a book of the Gospels, and it had been beautifully made. Somehow it got lost by being accidentally dropped into a river. Great efforts were made to find it, but unsuccessfully. Eventually it was found and it was not badly damaged. The finding and preservation of the book was considered miraculous and was attributed to Margaret's holiness. There is a Gospel book which belonged to Queen Margaret now kept in a library in Oxford University, which is considered to be probably but not certainly this particular book.

Margaret was a remarkable Christian wife and mother. She had eight children who were well instructed in the Christian faith. Her daughter Edith later married Henry 1 of England and became known as Good Queen Maud, for her holy ways. Her son Ethelred became an abbot. Her two youngest sons became kings of Scotland and it has been said that they carried on her policies. The youngest of these two sons, David, was canonised as a saint after he died. The next 200 years were called the "golden age" for Scotland. An amazing family record and one to be proud of!

St. Margaret died in 1093 at the age of only 47, several days after she heard of the death of her beloved husband and her son Edgar in battle. She had been seriously ill for a little while before this. All the time she was Queen, she never relaxed her efforts to try and do good for her adopted country, the country of her husband. She and her beloved husband were buried in Dunfermline Abbey, which immediately became a site for pilgrimages, such was her fame for saintliness. She was canonised in 1259. The reports of miracles occurring at the abbey just after her death no doubt hastened the canonisation. The faith and piety of many became stronger when they heard of the untimely death of their beloved, saintly queen.

A biography of Margaret was written by a monk named Turgot who knew her well. In it he wrote, "First of all, with the help of God, she made the King himself most attentive to works of justice, mercy, almsgiving and other virtues. Since he clearly perceived that Christ was truly dwelling in her heart, he hastened all the more quickly to obey her wishes and prudent counsels. What she refused he refused, and what she loved he loved for the love of her love". Concluding this biography, Turgot wrote, "Queen Margaret was a virtuous woman, and in the sight of God she showed herself to be a pearl, precious in faith and in works". It seems that those few words summed up perfectly the life of the saintly queen.

Endnotes

1. It is interesting to note that the father of King Malcolm 111 of Scotland, husband of Margaret, was King Duncan who was murdered by Macbeth, the same Macbeth whom Shakespeare had say in his famous play, before he carried out the murder, "If t'were done, then t'were well t'were done quickly". Malcolm was only a child when his father died.
2. The two places on the Firth of Forth between which the ferries sailed in the time of Queen Margaret and later on are named after her to this day. There is South Queensferry and North Queensferry.
3. The name Alexander was introduced into Scotland by Queen Margaret whose third son became King Alexander l of Scotland in 1107. This name was borne by three of the Scottish kings and became a national name.

Sources

Living with Christ. Calendar of Saints. (Novalis.Vol 34, Montreal, Canada 2010.)

Saints Alive by Anne Fremantle. (Doubleday & Company, New York, U.S.A.. 1978.)

Saints in due Season by Thomas P. McDonnell. (Our Sunday Visitor Inc., Huntington, Indiana, U.S.A. 1983.)

Saints. The Art, the History, the Inspiration by Michael McMahon. (MQ Publications Ltd., London, England. 2006.)

Saint Watching by Phyllis McGinley. (The Viking Press Inc., New York, U.S.A. 1969.)

Saints who spoke English by Leo Knowles. (Carillon Books, St. Paul, Minnesota, U.S.A.. 1979.)

The Brendan Voyage by Tim Severin. (Hutchinson & Co. Ltd., London, England. 1978.)

The Days of the Martyrs by C.Bernard Ruffin. (Our Sunday Visitor Inc., Huntington, Indiana, U.S.A. 1985.)

The Monastery of St. Albans by Gerald Sanctuary, St. Albans, Hertfordshire, England. 1980.

www.catholic.org/saints.

www.newadvent.org

www.wikipedia.org